The
UPSIDE
of Risk

The
UPSIDE
of Risk

Turning Complex Burdens into
Strategic Advantages for
Financial Institutions

By MICHAEL BERMAN

ISBN: 978-1-7374688-0-6 (Paperback)
ISBN: 978-1-7374688-1-3 (eBook)

Edited by Kelly Pike

Book and cover design by Katie Wetherby

First printing edition 2021

www.ncontracts.com

To my wife, April

Love is the risk that's always worth taking.
So glad you took a risk on me!

CONTENTS

FOREWORD

By Karl Nelson,
Founder and CEO of KPN Consulting
Faculty, Graduate School of Banking at Colorado

When I began my journey in this great industry way back in 1972, I was feeling pretty good about myself as I started with Chase Manhattan Bank in New York. Armed with my Bomar calculator, I knew I could quickly add and subtract my numbers without fear of error. That meant I could calculate credit risk, and that's all I was really concerned about.

What a simpler time!

As we work through our second Black Swan event of the past few years, it reminds me of how our concept of risk and risk management has evolved and the dramatic impact it has had on the financial industry.

I remember getting my first computer in my office at the Federal Home Loan Bank of Atlanta in the early 1990s. Finally, a place to hang my suit coat! I never would have guessed how that machine and the automation it brought would deliver unimaginable efficiencies and conveniences, but also increase risk. It's a trend that continues today as we enhance our businesses with new vendor partners, exposing ourselves to mounting risks.

Today, we are faced with a multitude of risks, making risk management a major concern for industry leaders. It's a major reason why we've lost nearly half of our FDIC-insured institutions in the past 20 years— and I suspect it will continue to drive the loss of many more institutions in the coming years. If there is one way to curb this consolidation within our industry, it is by creating a system for identifying and managing the risks that make our industry so interesting and so rewarding.

Unfortunately, too many bankers resist risk management. Regulators are often the ones pushing for enhanced risk management, and that often creates resistance from banking leadership. In my view, these are the leading contenders for losing their franchise. Our ideas about risk management are a work in progress. Regulators are working through this process themselves, and this can lead to faulty concepts that further alienate the industry. We are all in this together, and if we work together on the issue of enhancing our risk management processes, we will have the tools needed to ensure the survival and success of the industry.

There has never been a better time to work even harder on understanding and managing the risks in the banking industry. We have witnessed two major crises events since 2007. The first was self-inflicted. The desire to see more homeownership in this country was understandable since homeownership is the greatest source of household wealth in our society. However, wanting a specific outcome without proper regard for the risk is a recipe for disaster. The Great Recession taught us that abandoning basic risk parameters, including the need for buyers to have skin in the game and a real review of debt service capacity, is foolish. If we could take what was considered the gold standard for safe loans (the 30-year fixed-rate mortgage) and help almost destroy the U.S. economy, we really needed to get to the bottom of enhanced risk management.

This was followed by a (hopefully) once-in-a-lifetime pandemic in March 2020. Unlike the Great Recession, the pandemic was not self-inflicted, but the consequences were far reaching just the same. For the second time in less than 12 years, we were reminded that strategic planning and sound risk management are essential if we are to survive as an industry.

As a lifelong banker, I am very proud of our accomplishments during the past year. Bankers were instrumental in saving many businesses while providing immediate relief to those who would otherwise have been unemployed. Our efforts, in partnership with the Small Business

Administration, were truly a great reminder of what we can do when needed. We were responsible for much of the heavy lifting necessary to ensure economic recovery.

We didn't get everything right, though. While some elements of our pandemic response were the result of good planning, too many of us were simply reacting to the moment. Once again, we saw the results of not understanding risk. We'll be better prepared should another pandemic occur, but what about the next unexpected event? This experience has made us all more aware of the problems associated with a lack of risk management processes.

That's why I'm so excited to see this book. Michael Berman is one of the very best and most vocal voices in the industry when it comes to understanding risk. I've worked with Michael and his company, Ncontracts, since 2014. Since then, I've watched him elevate the discussion of risk in our industry. Tireless and wonderfully helpful, Michael explains how risk impacts our daily lives as bankers and then provides common-sense solutions for enhancing existing risk management processes. His ability to communicate with bankers is extraordinary, and this book is an extension of that capability.

As you read through each chapter, you will find that risk begins to take on a more immediate and clarified posture in your world. We learn how the historic silos we have built for risk management are helpful but fall short in understanding the entirety of enterprise risk management (ERM). Michael takes on each topic with a clear view of the steps needed to create the optimal program for your institution.

Somehow, he makes what could easily be a less-than-enthralling subject into a very relevant exploration of the next phase of risk management in the financial services industry. His book is filled with real-life examples of how failed risk management processes can damage an institution. These stories bring home in a very vivid way the dangers of not creating a sound ERM process at your institution.

This is the best and most descriptive view of enterprise risk management in print today. Make time to enjoy Michael's timely exploration of risk and risk management, and you will be well on your way to enhancing how you manage risk. More importantly, you will find new ways to ensure your own survival in the coming years.

INTRODUCTION

There's a flaw in just about every book about strategic planning I've ever read.

It's not that every book seems to talk about the same handful of Fortune 500 companies, though I'll admit the stories do get a little old. By now we all know that Southwest distinguishes itself as "the low-cost airline," Apple aims to dominate with simple, intuitive, and innovative designs, and Starbucks wants to "elevate and redefine the premium coffee experience." Message received loud and clear.

No, the problem isn't the companies. It's the conversation. Many books on strategic planning focus on vision, innovation, and inspiration, which encourages entrepreneurs and executives to seek out new answers to old questions. Others tackle practical, hands-on considerations like profits, assets, growth, and people. These are all important topics that contribute to strategic success.

Yet one critical element is commonly left out of the narrative: risk.

I'm not talking about the legend of how a company's founders spent their personal savings, maxed out credit cards, and borrowed money from their families, putting homes and retirement funds at stake, to start up. That's a personal risk, one that can have disastrous consequences

1

for one's finances and family relationships, but it is ultimately one small element of a much bigger picture.

When I talk about risk, I mean enterprise risk and the importance of having an ongoing process to assess, monitor, and control all risk within an organization to promote thoughtful decision making. It's knowing where both trouble and opportunity might lay and how it could affect the business.

Innovation, profits, assets, growth, and people are all critical elements of strategic planning. But to create the conditions necessary for success, risk must be a prominent factor. Strategic planning and risk management are not separate activities. They are intertwined, complementing each other like two wings on an airplane. Lose a wing and a plane simply can't fly.

Risk matters, and this is not just in a hypothetical or philosophical way. Properly managing risk can have a tangible impact on a company's bottom line. Companies with mature enterprise risk management (ERM) programs are valued 25 percent more than their peers, according to a study published in *The Journal of Risk and Insurance.*[1] "Firms that have successfully integrated the ERM process into both their strategic activities and everyday practices display superior ability in uncovering risk dependencies and correlations across the entire enterprise and as a consequence enhanced value when undertaking the ERM maturity journey," note the study's authors. Banks that embrace risk management are also more resilient, according the research by the Federal Reserve Bank of St. Louis.[2]

It makes sense that companies with a solid handle on risk are stronger and more valuable. The concept of risk has grown increasingly more complex and interrelated. Just one change in regulation, competition, or in the economy can have ripple effects touching many areas throughout an institution—from IT and operations to lending and marketing. Just consider the way the COVID-19 pandemic dramatically altered the risk management landscape. When 2020 began, the economy was on solid footing and financial institutions were anticipating another profitable year of business as usual. Those projections and estimates were rendered useless just a few months into the year as the economy was shuttered. Financial institutions scrambled to adapt as branches closed, employees worked from home, and the government passed new regulations to aid consumers struggling with illness, job loss, and other unforeseen circumstances. These changes required an all-hands-on deck effort that drew on the expertise of every department, including IT, human resources, lending, compliance, customer service, finance, audit, and operations. Institutions had to identify new areas of increased risk, asses those risks, and then map out how to mitigate them. At least, that's what the most successful ones did. They already knew that proper risk management cuts through silos. It creates a system that elevates awareness of risk throughout the enterprise and gauges its impact.

The goal of risk management isn't to eliminate risk. It's to understand it.

Strong risk management provides a financial institution's board and management with better information and tools which leads to more informed decision making. This book will show you how to make risk an important consideration in every decision your institution makes.

It begins by re-defining strategic success. Chapter 1 will explain the difference between strategy and strategic planning and the role risk management plays in reducing obstacles and maximizing opportunities for success. Risk management is no longer solely the domain of the chief financial officer. It requires interdisciplinary effort, aligning mission, vision, and values with strategy.

Risk takes many forms, and strategy without careful risk management isn't strategy. It's just a plan built on shaky assumptions.

Chapter 2 provides a primer on risk. You'll learn about the most common types of risk a financial institution faces, how to govern risk management, and how to balance risk and reward. I'll show you why risk needs to be examined on an enterprise-wide basis and how enterprise risk management creates value.

We'll take this discussion to the next level in Chapter 3 when I introduce the concept of enterprise risk management through the lens of the Committee of Sponsoring Organizations of the Treadway Commission's (COSO) updated ERM framework. COSO's *Enterprise Risk Management—Integrating with Strategy and Performance* is an essential piece of ERM reading. It shows us how best practices for ERM have evolved and how institutions must evolve along with them. We'll also consider what the federal supervisory agencies say about ERM and the consequences of failing to live up to their mandates.

Chapter 4 is all about identifying risk. We'll go through the steps of the risk assessment lifecycle before learning how to establish the context for a risk assessment. We'll discuss strategies for uncovering risks and illustrate common risks in three important areas. You'll see examples of why an institution must constantly be on the lookout for new, emerging, and evolving risks that could impact strategy.

Building on the COSO framework, Chapter 5 will demonstrate the importance of strong governance. Real-world examples will elucidate the dangers of failing to account for risk. I'll take you inside the reckless decision making that led to the failure of Washington Mutual and show you why poor risk management governance and oversight led to Wells Fargo's credit card scandal. We'll talk about what goes wrong and how to make it right.

After reviewing governance, Chapter 6 will explain how a risk management culture (or lack thereof) can support or sabotage an institution's strategic goals. I'll share the findings of an enterprise-wide study at Barclay's Bank to understand how culture played a role in its participation in the London Interbank Offered Rate (LIBOR) scandal. You'll learn about best practices in creating a culture of risk management and how that culture can add to your institution's bottom line.

Chapter 7 will teach you how to assess and measure risk, including inherent and residual risk. You'll learn how to create metrics that track known risks and suggest areas of potential risk. We'll talk about what makes an effective metric, how to structure oversight to create accountability, and the four most common mistakes institutions make when measuring risk. We'll also address why some controls are more effective than others and why some risks have greater impacts than others.

We'll then apply this knowledge in Chapter 8 by analyzing risk using two examples that are common in the financial services industry. You'll learn how to calculate inherent and residual risk to understand the relationship between the riskiness of an activity and the strength of the controls designed to mitigate that risk.

Chapter 9 is dedicated to audit and findings management. Independent auditors bring fresh eyes to the task of assessing the effectiveness of a risk management program and ensure processes and results are compliant and trustworthy. The best ones do it with a risk management mindset. I'll break down the five must-have elements of an effective audit program, offer insights on how to maximize audit resources, and explore how audits are evolving. You'll learn best practices for communicating audit findings and understand why findings are strategically important and what to do about it.

In Chapter 10, we'll bring it all together to learn how to apply risk management to setting strategy. I'll reveal the strategy setting missteps that prevent financial institutions from achieving success and show you the right way to set strategy. Examining potential strategy from a risk management perspective, you'll learn the types of questions to ask to understand the potential risks and benefits of a strategy and how to set measurable goals and objectives. I'll also show how to set a successful fintech strategy.

Finally, we'll wrap things up in Chapter 11 by talking about the biggest risk of all: doing nothing to address risk. You'll learn about some of the most common traps financial institutions fall into when they fail to think comprehensively about risk and the ways it costs them in dollars, time, and resources.

Read on to see how you can help your institution soar to new heights by effectively addressing risk.

CHAPTER ONE

STRATEGIC SUCCESS

Every strategy has risk, but not every risk is worth taking.

A ctions have consequences, and those consequences are often unexpected or unintended. It's common sense, and yet it's often ignored.

We are wired with an optimism bias.[3] Our brains are designed so that each of us believes that we are less likely than others to experience bad things and more likely to experience the good. We believe the lottery ticket we buy will be the winning one even though the odds are not in our favor. We assume that car accidents are something that happen to other people, that we'll live a long time, and that our children will be exceptional.

It's nice to live with hope. It makes us happier, but it doesn't necessarily make us more successful. Call me pessimistic, but I believe that the key to strategic success lies in the recognition that things aren't always so rosy. *We always need to consider risk.*

In fact, I would contend that a keen understanding of risk is the secret sauce missing from many strategic plans.

It begins with strategy. Strategy is a high-level plan designed to achieve one or more goals. Strategy involves setting goals and determining the actions necessary to achieve those goals.

A strategy is not strategic planning. Strategic planning is the process of defining strategy and making decisions about allocating resources to pursue this strategy. It's the difference between having an idea and having a plan.

A strategic plan is no guarantee of success. The plan is only as good as the research and due diligence that goes into it. An institution needs to understand its opportunities and challenges, both in the marketplace and within the institution itself, and how to overcome or exploit them to gain competitive advantages. It needs to be honest about the problems it faces and develop practical, real-world approaches to tackling them. It needs to consider the role of innovation. It needs to understand risk.

DEFINING STRATEGIC SUCCESS

The biggest obstacle to strategic success is failing to understand risk. A thorough risk management program includes voices from across the institution working together to recognize likely pitfalls and consider ways to avoid them by designing and implementing controls to mitigate the inherent risk. Risk management invites ideas from all areas of the institution, revealing potential weaknesses and also hidden strengths. An in-depth approach to risk management not only mitigates the probability or impact of unfortunate events, it also helps maximize the realization of opportunities.

Strategic success is the identification, assessment, and prioritization of risks followed by coordinated and economical application of resources to minimize, monitor, and mitigate the probability and/or impact of unfortunate events or maximize the realization of opportunities. It's having systems in place to measure and monitor risk and using that data to adjust plans and controls as needed.

Strategic success isn't just about *how*, it's about *why*.

Strategic Success

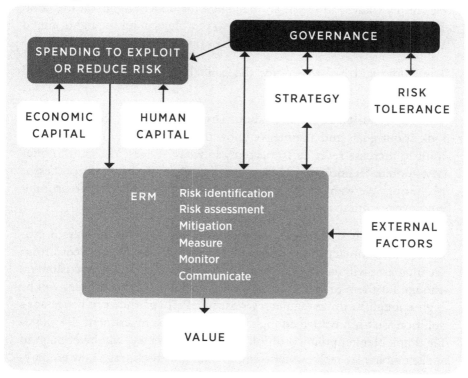

It reminds me of a story Shelly Palmer, CEO of The Palmer Group, told in *AdAge*[4] about a blue disco ball. Palmer was once a gofer on a movie set. His job was to get whatever was needed. One day the director told him he needed a 60-inch blue disco ball for an upcoming scene. Gofers don't ask why, they just do as they are told, so he set about on an exhaustive search of Hollywood. With no 60-inch blue disco balls in sight, he got permission to custom order one from a vendor at an astronomical cost of $10,000, which today is about $36,000.

On the day of the shoot, the delivery was running late, and the director was getting angry. When the studio's prop master came by and asked what the problem was the director said he needed a "huge" disco ball. Then the prop master asked a very good question: "What are you trying to accomplish?"

It turns out the director wasn't planning on including the ball in the shot. He simply wanted to see small "dancing blue dots of light" on the floor. The prop master instructed his team to put blue gel on the lights aimed at a silver disco ball, accomplishing the same affect for next to nothing.

The studio still had to pay for the ball, though, which was delivered shortly after.

This story can teach us a lot about strategic planning. Sometimes we look at our goals and assume we know the solution to our problem. We want to increase revenue 10 percent, so we raise fees. We want to offer new mobile technologies, so we just use whatever our core processor is offering. We want to control our image in the public, so we prohibit employees from using social media even in their off hours.

Are these the best choices? They may be, but there is no way of estimating their impact without considering risk. Maybe the blowback from fee increases will damage the institution's reputation or anger customers enough for them to look for a new place to bank. Maybe the fees will be high enough to draw regulatory scrutiny. Perhaps the core processor's solution isn't innovative enough to be worth the investment. It's possible that a blanket policy prohibiting social media use will be enough to make employees seek out new employment or discourage new employees from coming aboard in an industry with a shortage of top talent. You don't know if you don't take the time to ask.

You also want to ask the right people. Too often an institution blows the opportunity to plan ahead and talk about critical issues when all the institution's best and brightest minds are in the room because no one took the time to do the homework in advance. I'm sure there were plenty of meetings about sets, props, and costumes long before the director even stepped on a sound stage. You'd have thought that someone would have gone through the script and drafted a list of props, special effects, and other needs specifically mentioned in the script. Had someone taken notice of the "dancing blue dots of light" early on, it would have been brought up in a meeting with the prop master with decades of experience instead of being addressed last minute by a director with other talents, priorities, and concerns. It would have saved $10,000 and hours of the gofer's time as he called every prop house in town in search of an unnecessary and very specific 60-inch blue disco ball. After all, wouldn't a 59-inch disco ball have worked too?

I don't know what movie was being filmed or how it performed at the box office, but if the blue disco ball is any indicator of how the picture was produced, I doubt it was a strategic success. Clearly there were gaping holes in any coordinated effort or economical application of resources to limit negative events or realize opportunities.

ACHIEVING STRATEGIC SUCCESS

Strategic success happens when vision, mission, and values align with strategy, strategic objectives, and risk.

STRATEGIC PLANNING SUCCESS

What does this mean? First, we must define the terms.

Mission: A description of the institution's business, including what it aims to accomplish and how it aims to accomplish it. In short, it's why the institution exists. A mission statement is a roadmap for helping set priorities and objectives and allocate resources.

An example: *We will provide exemplary personalized financial services in our market, delivering value to shareholders, customers, employees, and the local community.*

Used as a guide, this particular mission statement favors decisions that support high levels of personal service and reminds decision makers that the impact on shareholders, customers, employees, and the community should be taken into consideration. If a proposed project or plan doesn't meet these standards, it needs to be rethought.

Vision: The institution's goals for the future. It's the destination.

An example: *Our dependable, customer-centric institution will be the area's leading small business lender, known for helping consumers, business owners, and the local community achieve financial success while rewarding employees and shareholders.*

Every decision the board, management, or employees make should support the vision. If, using the aforementioned vision statement as an example, a project introduces unreliable elements, draws employee attention away from serving customers, or pulls resources away from small business lending, it may not be a smart move. Similarly, every potential project should be assessed by how effective it will be in serving the goals of helping consumers, business owners, the community, employees, and shareholders. When a decision conflicts with that vision, it's a poor decision.

Values: The fundamental beliefs and ideals of the institution. This serves as a guidepost that helps the institution determine what is right or wrong when making both big picture and everyday decisions. While every business should run ethically, a financial institution's core values should reflect the essence of the institution. These vary from organization to organization.

Examples include: *sustainability, innovation, philanthropy, commitment, dependability, efficiency, open-mindedness, compassion, passion, positivity, respect, and stability.*

A financial institution that chooses innovation and open-mindedness as core values would make decisions that put it on the leading, if not bleeding, edge of technology. That would not necessarily be an appropriate choice for an institution that values dependability or stability. That institution would be far more likely to opt for tried-and-true strategies and only adopt a technology after it has proof of concept.

An institution's core values are not a wish list. They should be embedded and fostered within the existing culture. They are not something that can be overlooked for convenience, but part of the institution's fabric and one of the things that make the organization unique.

History tells us this isn't always the case. Remember Enron, the Houston-based energy company that went bankrupt in 2001, losing investors and employees billions of dollars? (More on them later.) At the time, it was the largest bankruptcy in U.S. history and the company's collapse epitomized the corporate fraud and scandals that rocked the first half of the 2000s. The company fell apart after executives manipulated earnings and stock prices and hid debt. Enron's 2000 annual report described the company's key values as communication, respect, integrity, and excellence.[5] Yet CEO Kenneth Lay was the opposite of respect, integrity, and excellence, at least according to the jury that found him guilty of 10 counts of conspiracy and securities fraud in 2006.[6]

Perhaps juror Wendy Vaughn said it best. A fellow business owner, Vaughn said she admired Lay and former CEO Jeffrey Skilling's business acumen and how they built up the business but noted "it was sad to see in the end, it wasn't accomplished in a respectful manner."[7]

And Lay was just one of many. In the end, 16 Enron executives were convicted[8] including Lay, Skilling, ex-chief financial officer Andrew Fastow, and ex-treasurer Ben Glisan.

BRINGING MISSION, VISION, AND VALUES TOGETHER

Mission, vision, and values can't stand alone. They are essential elements that set the tone for an institution and inform all strategic decisions. Not only do they influence overall decisions, but they interplay with each other to help an institution understand what type of business it is and what it stands for. Vision informs the mission. Values support how both mission and vision are to be accomplished.

That's where strategy, strategic objectives, and risk enter the picture. The mission, vision, and values of an institution aren't a platitude or a public relations exercise. They are the guiding force behind strategy and strategic objectives. Whenever the board or management makes a decision, it should take the institution one step closer to its mission and vision. It should also align with the institution's values. A strategy must be backed by carefully thought-out strategic objectives. Those strategic objectives must be selected based on a wide variety of factors, including risk. Once risk is understood, actions can be taken to forward the strategy and mitigate risk.

For example, an institution might consider a strategy of adopting faster or real-time payments. This could be a smart move for an organization that values innovation, with the vision to become a fintech leader and a mission to provide customers with cutting-edge services. It may not make business sense for an organization that values stability and aims to be the market leader for mortgage originations. An organization that values efficiency would have to determine whether providing customers the efficiency of faster payments is worth the expenditure of resources that could raise overhead costs.

The same conversation is necessary if an opportunity arises to open a bank branch or a loan production office in a distant location. If, after careful deliberation, the board has decided the bank's mission, vision, and values all involve focusing extensively on the local community, it may not be a good strategy or use of resources to open a branch in a different state. For a bank with the desire for a diverse geographic footprint, it's a much easier decision.

Before any decision can be made an institution needs to understand risk and how failing to align strategy and strategic objectives with mission, vision, and values introduces risk.

Let's say that the financial institution that values stability and wants to be the market leader for mortgage origination decides to go ahead with the faster payments strategy even though it doesn't appear to support its mission, vision, and values. The idea of faster payments is exciting and supports evolving customer expectations, but it will require resources. That means there will be fewer resources available to market, originate, close, and service mortgages while ensuring compliance. If a core update is necessary, the driving force behind that update may be faster payments instead of how it will support mortgages. Also, the newer technology is more likely to face hiccups than one that has been around for a decade, which could impact reliability. On the other hand, it may give the bank a competitive advantage if it can shave time off closing.

The only way to predict the results with any certainty is to fully assess these risks and opportunities to determine if the potential cost makes sense in light of the institution's mission, vision, and values. It needs to know how much potential risk exists and whether it aligns with the institution's risk tolerance, or the maximum amount of risk an institution is willing to expose itself to. Not only that, it must measure those results against other potential strategies to see if a strategy with less risk is more appropriate. Every strategy has risk, but not every risk is worth taking. By aligning risk with strategic planning, a financial institution is not just ensuring that its strategic decisions align with its mission, vision, and values, it aids in integrating the whole process to illuminate potential hazards and rewards so that an institution can follow its destiny in the most intelligent way possible.

CHAPTER TWO

WHAT IS RISK?

The overlapping nature of risk makes it essential for financial institutions to have a comprehensive, top-down approach to enterprise risk management.

Risk is not a four-letter word. It's a natural and sometimes even a desirable by-product of business.

All business decisions come with some degree of inherent risk. A business must decide if the opportunity for gains outweighs the risk. The key is to balance the potential for losses and gains while positioning the institution to withstand the shock of unexpected events.

The maxim of "no risk, no reward" rings true, but that doesn't mean that risk can be entered into haphazardly. To the contrary, risk is only worth undertaking when it has been carefully identified, assessed, measured, mitigated, and controlled as part of a deliberate strategy.

At its simplest, risk is the probability of a loss. Nearly every financial institution activity poses some kind of risk. A customer might fail to pay back a loan. Systems can be hacked. An oversight can result in a compliance violation.

But just because an activity has inherent risk doesn't mean it's not worth pursuing. Risk management is the process of methodically addressing potential risks tied to a specific activity to maximize the benefit of the activity by working to reduce risk. Enterprise risk management (ERM) ties these activities together to look at risk broadly across the institution to ensure its overall strategic decisions fall within its risk tolerance. Effective governance balances strategic planning with risk management to ensure an institution enters into new businesses, products, and systems with its eyes wide open.

When an institution carefully assesses risk, it understands where it has advantages over the competition that it can exploit, such as more market knowledge, greater flexibility, or superior technology. It also knows where there are weaknesses that need to be mitigated.

TYPES OF RISK

To properly manage risk, you have to understand what it looks like. In simpler times, risk was mainly the purview of the chief financial officer. Financial and credit risk were top of mind and the two biggest concerns a financial institution faced. Today risk is a multi-faceted concept that touches every aspect of a financial institution.

The most common types of risk include:

Operational risk. Operational risk is the risk of financial loss when processes, people, or systems fail. Sometimes it's the result of external events like a power outage, fire, or flood. Other times it's internal issues, such as fraud, a hardware or software failure, or an accounting error.

Transaction risk. Transaction risk is the risk that products and services won't be delivered as expected, adversely impacting the institution or its customers. Transaction risk differs from operational risk in that it focuses on contingency planning, but the two overlap in many areas.

Sometimes networks go down. Yet whether an outage or other business problem is caused by a natural disaster, cyberattack, equipment failure, fraud, or other event, institutions *must* have plans and procedures in place to ensure service and product delivery is quickly restored.

Compliance risk. Financial institutions must follow laws, regulations, and rules. Compliance risk is the risk that an institution will violate one of these orders or fail to follow the institution's own internal policies. This can have reputational, financial, and regulatory consequences for the financial institution.

Credit risk. Credit risk is the risk that a borrower fails to repay a loan, resulting in a financial loss to the institution.

Strategic risk. Strategic risk is the possibility that a company doesn't make decisions that support its long-term goals. This can happen when risks aren't properly assessed; not enough thought and due diligence are put into new products, business lines, or activities; or when the company undertakes an action that's not consistent with the company's goals or doesn't provide the expected return on investment.[9]

Strategic risk impacts the viability of a business in the same way credit risk does. But instead of focusing simply on numbers, it involves reviewing how decisions are made and implemented and how a company responds to changing market conditions. A company that isn't managed well may not stay in business long or provide quality products and services.

Reputation risk. Reputation is hard to earn and easy to lose. Lawsuits, fraud, service interruptions, data breaches, and other headline-worthy mistakes can erode customer trust and diminish the appeal of a business. Just think of the Target data breach in 2013 that affected 41 million customer payment card accounts and exposed contact information for more than 60 million customers. People are still talking about it and holding up the retailer as a cautionary tale.

Cyber risk. In a world of increasingly sophisticated cyber threats, it's essential that institutions have the ability to prevent, detect, and respond to cyberattacks. Cyber risk is about having the tools, policies, and procedures to identify and mitigate internal and external cyber threats and vulnerabilities.

Third-party risk. Financial institutions that outsource to third parties are just as responsible for actions that a vendor takes on the institution's behalf as those the institution performs itself. Third-party risk is the risk that a vendor or other third party poses to the institution.

Concentration risk. Concentration risk is the risk that an institution has taken on a significant amount of risk in a single facet of its business. Examples include lending to too many businesses in a single type of business or industry, making too many of the same type of loans (such as mortgages or commercial real estate), or relying on vendors all located in the same geographic area, creating the risk that they could all be impacted by the same disaster.

UNCOVERING RISK

With so many types of risk, it raises the question of what financial institutions need to do to strategically mitigate these risks. The answer is to periodically assess each business line, product, service, or system against each risk category to identify key risk drivers.

It may seem like a daunting task, but with a systematic approach the task becomes easier and more efficient over time, allowing an institution to see not just the risks in a particular activity, but how those risks intersect with others throughout the institution.

Here are just a few of the multitude of risk-related questions an institution should be asking.

- Do you have concentration issues?
- What can go wrong in your processes?
- How can fraud occur in your business?
- What might interrupt your business processes? System outages? Phone outages?
- What project and change risk are happening in your business?
- Do you have high-risk customers in your portfolio? If so, how are they managed?
- What key regulations govern your business?
- Are there other governing bodies to consider?
- What are your revenue goals?
- Have you been successful in reaching desired market share?
- What other risk categories apply to your business?

This list of questions is by no means exhaustive. It's only to illustrate that risk discussions must go way beyond a single risk manager or group. Answering these questions requires the expertise and input of managers and employees throughout the financial organization.

As regulatory guidance has expanded the scope of regulations over the past few years, the overlap between different areas of risk management has grown significantly. Enterprise risk management, business continuity planning, compliance, cybersecurity, and vendor management can no longer be thought of as stand-alone elements of a financial institution's operational risk management program because they are intertwined.

Consider security breaches of critical vendors, a regulatory hot topic. It's so hot, in fact, that it touches five areas of risk management:

1. **Vendor management.** Regulators want institutions to know if critical vendors are required to provide notice if there's a security breach

2. **Cybersecurity.** The FFIEC's Cybersecurity Assessment Tool specifically asks if all critical vendors are required by contract to notify the financial institution when there is a security breach.

3. **Business continuity planning.** An institution should know how long it will take critical vendors to notify the institution of a security breach.

4. **Compliance.** The Gramm-Leach-Bliley Act specifically mentions that vendors with access to protected data should be required to notify the financial institution of a security breach.

5. **Enterprise risk management.** A financial institution needs to determine if critical vendors are required to notify the institution of a security breach.

In theory, overlapping requirements like these should make risk management simpler for financial institutions. One person or team can address these concerns and report back to everyone who needs the information.

But that's not always what happens.

Too often financial institutions rely on a decentralized approach to risk management. The IT department handles cybersecurity, compliance tackles vendor management, and someone else in IT oversees business continuity planning. The result is silos. Each team meticulously follows regulatory requirements and best practices for risk management, but they never consider the possibility that someone else at the financial institution may be tackling a similar task.

While this might have worked in the past when there was less overlap, today a siloed approach to risk management results in redundancies, inefficiencies, and discrepancies.

Redundancies. In the security breach example, there may be as many as five different groups compiling lists of third-party vendors, assessing the criticality of individual vendors, and determining which vendors should report breaches and when. When it comes time to test controls, each control is tested five times instead of simply testing it once and sharing the findings with everyone involved. This repetition isn't thoroughness. It is just a waste of time and resources.

Inefficiencies. There can also be as many as five teams monitoring and setting policy for security breaches of critical vendors. Instead of working cooperatively to maximize knowledge and resources, each group starts from scratch. The compliance department doesn't benefit from IT's knowledge of cybersecurity. The vendor management and contract teams don't necessarily understand the expectations of business continuity planning. Enterprise risk management isn't providing the overall leadership needed to make the process function smoothly. It's a waste of expertise.

Discrepancies. When different groups unknowingly have overlapping responsibilities, it can create conflict as each group sets different standards and notification times. For instance, the IT team may require breach notification within one hour, while compliance may say 24 hours. These kinds of discrepancies are red flags for regulators.

The overlapping nature of risk makes it essential for financial institutions to have a comprehensive, top-down approach to enterprise risk management. By taking a broad view of risk management, institutions can leverage the risk assessment and mitigation work performed by various departments throughout the institution, streamlining the process to make it more effective and more efficient.

ERM should serve as an umbrella for all other areas of risk management, developing systems that connect all areas so that every requirement can be studied from multiple perspectives. Not only does this ensure business strategies are integrated into every risk decision, it also creates a central hub where risk management can be viewed holistically.

With silos eliminated, risk management becomes more effective. Departments build on and leverage each other's work, which results in better oversight, greater efficiency, and lower costs.

UNDERSTANDING ERM

At its simplest, ERM is a system to manage risk. It examines risk holistically to understand how different areas of the institution interconnect. It's about identifying, assessing, mitigating, measuring, monitoring, and communicating risk. The goal of ERM isn't just to identify risks to exploit or reduce them. It's also to create value.

A lot of institutions employ *risk management* but fail to fully implement *enterprise risk management*. What's the difference? Risk management uses a rifle approach, shooting one thing at a time. It's the risk management equivalent of the carnival game Whack-A-Mole. A problem pops up, you knock it out and move on to the next one.

ERM is a team sport. Success depends on every player (or in this case, every department, function, or business line) contributing their knowledge and skills. While each one has a specific role and set of duties, no one operates on an island. They all depend on each other.

This is especially true at financial institutions. Every department depends on other departments. Deposit operations might rely on accounting, IT, and maybe even lending if it takes applications.

Risk Management Defined

The Institute of Risk Management describes risk management as "a central part of any organization's strategic management. It is the process whereby organizations methodically address the risks attaching to their activities with the goal of achieving sustained benefit within each activity and across the portfolio of all activities."[10]

In a study of ERM in banks published by the *ACCMAN Journal of Management,* ERM is "the discipline, by which an organization in any industry assesses, controls, exploits, finances, and monitors risks from all sources for the purpose of increasing the organizations short- and long-term value to stakeholders."[11]

ERM AND BUSINESS CONTINUITY MANAGEMENT (BCM)

A good business continuity plan needs to uncover an institution's interdependencies to understand what functions an organization needs. For instance, every plan should have recovery time objectives (RTOs) and recovery point objectives (RPOs) that determine when a function must get back online and to what point in time it must be restored. These RTOs and RPOs often depend on an interdependent function with an RTO and RPO of its own. If accounting has an RTO of 12 hours, and deposit operations depends on the accounting function, deposit operations isn't going to be able to restore operations in 6 hours. Each area needs to understand and account for these interdependencies.

Vendor management is a critical part of business continuity planning. An institution needs to know which third parties it will rely on to help get back to business. This includes regular vendors needed to operate in a business-as-usual environment as well as vendors who may aid in recovery, such as providers of environmental services or emergency supplies like generators. If vendor management isn't represented in business continuity planning, there will be substantial holes in the plan, limiting its ability to mitigate the risks of a crisis.

Compliance risk is another major risk addressed by ERM. While the compliance department oversees compliance, everyone at the financial institution is responsible for following the policies and procedures that ensure compliance. From fair lending and vendor management to IT security and adequate management oversight, compliance risk will increase if the compliance department doesn't have ways to communicate, train on, delegate responsibility for, monitor, and document compliant and noncompliant actions. ERM makes it possible for compliance to determine where compliance risk is greatest and allocate its limited resources to the areas of greatest concern.

But how does an institution do this? Let's revisit the diagram for strategic success from Chapter 1 to find out.

Strategic Success

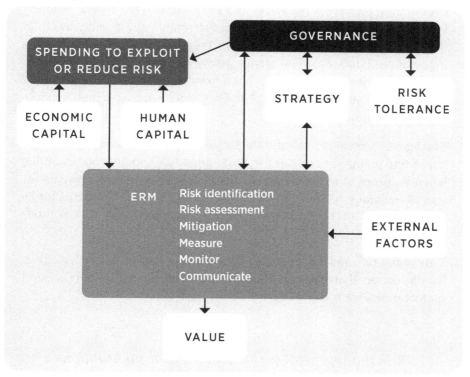

It begins at the top with governance. The board and management are responsible for setting strategy that aligns with the institution's mission, vision, and values. Part of that is determining the institution's risk tolerance in the form of a risk appetite statement.

A risk appetite statement is the amount of risk an entity is willing to take on to achieve its mission, goals, and strategic objectives. This may vary from category to category of risk. It also varies widely by institution and by industry. For example, an institution may be comfortable with moderate technology or vendor risk but quite conservative and tolerate only low risk when it comes to lending or compliance. These reasons should be documented so it's easy to understand why a decision was made and can help future assessors.

Consider the OCC. While the OCC is conservative by nature and its overarching priority is the safety and soundness of the federal banking system, in its Enterprise Risk Appetite Statement[12] the agency says it "is willing to assume certain risks to remain nimble," especially in an evolving financial landscape. The agency assesses nine risk categories, breaking each area into areas where it has a low risk appetite and areas where it has a moderate risk appetite. (The OCC does not have a high appetite for risk in any area.)

The agency's review dives into the details, separately assessing subcategories and giving the reasons for its assigned risk appetite. For example, when it comes to technology risk, the OCC has a low risk appetite for lack of resiliency against cybersecurity threats, but its risk appetite for its ability to meet user demands and support a mobile workforce is moderate.

This shows risk management isn't a simple yes or no situation. It's a careful discussion that balances safety and soundness with flexibility and opportunities for innovation.

Risk management isn't a simple yes or no situation. It's a careful discussion that balances safety and soundness with flexibility and opportunities for innovation.

RISK VERSUS REWARD: FINDING A BALANCE IN A RISK APPETITE STATEMENT

Risk management is about identifying and preventing loss. Every dollar an institution doesn't lose is essentially one dollar gained. But that doesn't mean there isn't a place for risk when it is carefully assessed and measured.

Every institution needs to understand its overall appetite for risk and include it as a consideration when making strategic decisions. It's not just about nothing ventured, nothing gained. It's deciding how much venture is worth a potential gain or loss.

This is more than a philosophy. An institution's risk appetite should be determined by the board and then translated into a written document, including policies and procedures that can guide the institution in its strategy setting and decision making. There are many ways to draft a risk appetite statement, but at its core it should serve as a guide for strategic decision making and resource allocation.

For instance, a risk appetite statement can outline whether an institution has a low, moderate, or high tolerance for risk in several key categories such as lending, technology, or operational risk. Any new proposed activity should be risk assessed to see whether it falls within tolerance limits. Those activities that are viewed as riskier, but within limits, can be allocated additional resources for measuring and monitoring risk (more on this in Chapter 4).

That's why it's essential to look at risk strategically. While too many big banks have made headlines and nearly toppled the financial system by ignoring risk, some institutions are on the opposite end of the risk spectrum. They fall short of their potential by passing up opportunities due to the perceived risk without ever delving into the details. They make strategic decisions based on snap assumptions and gut reactions instead of careful assessments. Whether its marketplace lending or innovations in payments, these off-the-cuff assumptions about why a product or service won't work can be just as dangerous as automatically assuming that they will.

How many institutions put off adopting mobile check deposit because the very idea scared them? Many of these institutions didn't take the time to understand the potential risk and rewards of the technology, assuming that fraud would pose too much of a barrier. That gave other institutions a leg up in adopting the technology, wooing customers enchanted by the idea of depositing checks quickly and easily with the device that's always in their pocket. It was a lost opportunity that likely resulted in losing customers lured away by convenience. Those customers aren't coming back.

It also proved to be a disadvantage when the COVID-19 pandemic caused widespread branch closures throughout the country. Institutions that didn't offer mobile banking apps or those who had clunky outdated apps scrambled to catch up so that consumers stuck at home could manage their finances from their couches. Institutions had to quickly onboard a new vendor, implement the technology, and then find ways to let consumers know they had it. In some cases, they also had to train consumers on how to use it. Had this technology been adopted in advance, these institutions would have had more time to think about long-term strategy when selecting a mobile banking vendor. This may include everything from growth to planned core upgrades. They would have had time to demonstrate the technology in-branch to consumers who needed assistance. Consumers would have had the ability to deposit a check from the safety of their own homes at the beginning of the pandemic when uncertainty was greatest.

Missed opportunities are deadly. But ignoring risk is worse.

IT ALL COMES BACK TO ERM

A carefully calibrated risk tolerance is essential to success, helping to inform strategy, but it's useless without tools to measure and monitor risk.

That's where ERM comes in. ERM identifies, assesses, mitigates, measures, monitors, and communicates risk across an institution. This provides essential feedback to the board and management. It provides the knowledge needed to ascertain whether a business activity falls within an institution's risk tolerance and regularly monitors internal and external factors to alert the institution of any changes.

In an evolving threat landscape with changing economic conditions, a risk assessment may lose its relevance over time. ERM ensures that risks are continually managed by regularly monitoring and adjusting risk assessments. External factors can be economic, regulatory, political, environmental, market-related, technological, legal, and financial, among others. Trends in corporate governance and best practices can also play a role. Not every change will require a full risk assessment revision. Sometimes it's enough to just note a growing trend and keep an eye on it. Regular monitoring prevents mission creep, where strategy shifts over time, rendering risk assessments obsolete.

ERM also aids in developing and executing strategies to mitigate potential risks, helping the board and management decide where to spend limited economic and human capital resources. In a world with limited resources, it is necessary to understand whether a risk control is effective and how much impact it has on an institution to justify the expense. For instance, if an institution is making a large investment in a control for a low-risk activity, those resources may be better deployed on a high-risk activity. Similarly, an assessment may determine that a control is not particularly effective and should be discontinued.

Ultimately, ERM creates value by uncovering opportunities and threats, optimizing resource use, helping an institution stay abreast of current conditions, and ensuring the promotion of strategies that support the institution's mission, vision, and values.

CHAPTER THREE

A FRAMEWORK FOR ERM

ERM needs to be hard-wired and ingrained into an institution's structure. It's not an add-on, but fundamental to the organization's existence. Take one component away, and the whole structure unravels.

Before an institution can begin to uncover threats and opportunities, it needs to have an enterprise risk management framework in place. An ERM framework is a high-level foundational document outlining how an institution plans to manage risk.

There's no shortage of ERM frameworks. There's the ISO 31000 series and the NIST Risk Management Framework, among others, but the leading framework used by financial institutions comes from The Committee of Sponsoring Organizations of the Treadway Commission (COSO). You'll understand why it's so valuable as soon as you see the title: Enterprise Risk Management—Integrating with Strategy and Performance.

There it is, strategy and risk management tied all together and backed by extensive research. When updating its framework in 2017, COSO held meetings around the world with industry practitioners, academia, government agencies, and non-profit organizations, conducted an in-depth survey, and sought public comment before updating the framework. Now it's a must-read for every business executive. Organized into five parts, the framework offers a blueprint for ensuring risk is addressed on a continuum at every level of an organization.

Enterprise Risk Management

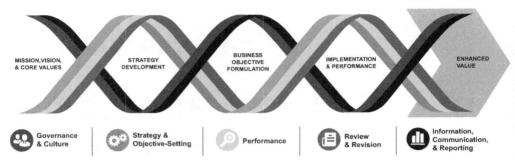

Source: COSO's Enterprise Risk Management—Integrating with Strategy and Performance.

Compared to the previous version (Enterprise Risk Management—Integrated Framework, published in 2004) today's COSO framework does much more to integrate risk into the strategic planning process. The framework "positions risk in the context of an organization's performance, rather than as the subject of an isolated exercise" and "enables organizations to better anticipate risk so they can get ahead of it, with an understanding that change creates opportunities, not simply the potential for crises."[13]

How does it do this? Let's take a closer look at the diagram above to understand.

We've already talked about the role risk plays in ensuring that an institution's mission, vision, and values influence an institution's strategy, strategic plan, and ultimately its strategic success. But ERM goes far deeper than that. As COSO explains, "Enterprise risk management is not a function or department. It is the culture, capabilities, and practices that organizations integrate with strategy-setting and apply when they carry out that strategy, with the purpose of managing risk in creating, preserving, and realizing value."

When addressed properly, ERM should be entwined in every step of a strategic plan.

The COSO framework divides the components and principles of an effective ERM program into five categories:

- Governance & Culture
- Strategy & Objective-Setting
- Performance
- Review & Revision
- Information, Communication & Reporting

Notice how these components are banded together in ribbons that wrap around they key steps of developing and executing a business strategy. The design resembles the double helix structure of DNA, a nod to the idea that ERM needs to be hard-wired and ingrained into an institution's structure. It's not an add-on, but fundamental to the organization's existence. Take one component away, and the whole structure unravels.

COSO'S ERM COMPONENTS

Let's take a deeper look at what COSO expects from ERM.

Governance & Culture

Governance and culture are all about responsibility. It addresses who is in charge of risk management and how ethics will be applied. Components include:

1. Exercising board risk oversight
2. Establishing operating structure
3. Defining desired culture
4. Demonstrating commitment to core values
5. Attracting, developing, and retaining capable individuals

Strategy & Objective-Setting

This is where the rubber meets the road and risk management, strategy, and objective setting occur in tandem to develop a strategic plan. This includes adopting a risk appetite appropriate for the institution's strategy, selecting business objectives, and having a method in place to identify, assess, and react to risk. Components include:

1. Analyzing business context

2. Defining risk appetite

3. Evaluating alternative strategies

4. Formulating business objectives

Performance
In this case performance isn't about year-end financial reports. It's how well the institution identifies, assesses, prioritizes, and remediates risks that impact performance and the ability of the institution to achieve its objectives. Components include:

1. Identifying risk

2. Assessing severity of risk

3. Prioritizing risks

4. Implementing risk responses

5. Developing portfolio view

Review & Revision
The world is constantly changing and so are the risks faced by an institution. This phase ensures an institution is regularly monitoring the environment for new risks, changes in current risks, the control environment, and the effectiveness of controls, and improvements to its overall ERM program. Components include:

1. Assessing substantial change

2. Reviewing risk and performance

3. Pursuing improvement in enterprise risk management

Information, Communication & Reporting
Siloes are the enemy of ERM. The board's decisions about risk appetite and strategic goals must be shared with the rest of the institution. Employees need to share their work in ERM with management. Departments must work together to increase efficiency when responsibilities overlap and to identify risks before they spread. Information must be shared regularly. Components include:

1. Leveraging information systems

2. Communicating risk information

3. Reporting on risk, culture, and performance

COSO's ERM framework is not a one-size-fits-all solution. It's designed to be useful to organizations and institutions of all sizes, from a $120 million-asset community bank to one the size of Bank of America. The beauty of the framework is that it provides flexibility when needed. For instance, it doesn't demand a risk committee or a risk officer, it provides recommendations for the type of work that needs to be done. It's also firm when necessary, specifically when it comes to ensuring that ethics and core values are followed. It doesn't offer loopholes when it comes to doing the right thing.

The Origins of COSO

You're probably familiar with COSO. Founded in 1985, COSO is a private-sector initiative originally formed to combat fraudulent financial reporting but has expanded its mission over the years to include internal controls and enterprise risk management. COSO is sponsored by the American Accounting Association, the American Institute of Certified Public Accountants, Financial Executives International, The Institute of Internal Auditors, and the Institute of Management Accountants.

COSO provides guidance on best practices. In addition to its ERM framework, it also published the Internal Control – Integrated Framework in 1992. COSO's internal control framework was a big deal when it was first published. It offered companies of all sizes a new way of looking at internal controls, one that shifted responsibility for these functions to the board and senior management. It was meant to be integrated and comprehensive, eliminating silos and adding transparency and greater oversight. The framework has evolved since that time, with an update in 2015 to reflect changes in today's business and operating environment and our increased dependence on information technology, among other advances in governance,[14] but it still comes down to five components for effective internal controls:

- **Control environment.** These are the "standards, processes, and structures" the board and senior management create to ensure internal controls are followed. These include oversight and responsibility, performance measures, and accountability.
- **Risk assessment.** Identifying and assessing risks and their impact on business objectives and their suitability.
- **Control activities.** Documented actions dictated by policy and procedure that ensure risks are mitigated.

- **Information and communication.** Enterprise-wide communication in all directions to ensure internal and external information is shared in a timely fashion.
- **Monitoring activities.** Evaluations to ensure the first four components are properly executed.

Many regulators have endorsed COSO, including the Federal Deposit Insurance Corporation (FDIC), the Federal Reserve, and the OCC. They have "encouraged [institutions] to evaluate their internal control against the COSO framework.[15] The National Credit Union Administration (NCUA) describes COSO as "the internal control framework most often cited"[16] by credit unions. It's not just popular in financial circles. With the support of entities like the Securities and Exchange Commission (SEC), the COSO framework has seen widespread adoption. While COSO standards are optional, they are widely used at most publicly traded companies. One consulting firm's study found that in 2015, 75 percent of publicly traded companies had adopted the 2013 COSO internal control framework and 17 percent were still using the 1992 version.[17]

ENRON AND THE EVOLUTION OF ERM

As with most guidance and regulation, COSO's ERM framework was inspired by a scandal. In this case, it was the slew of accounting scandals and corporate bankruptcies, including Enron, Tyco International, WorldCom, and many others in the early 2000s. Energy company Enron was one of the 10 largest companies in the U.S., with over $60 billion in assets, when it collapsed and declared bankruptcy in December 2001. Investors saw share prices plummet from $90 in August 2000 to less than 10 cents just over a year later, causing investors to lose an estimated $11 billion. Tyco International followed in July 2002 after executives embezzled about $600 million. WorldCom eclipsed Enron's bankruptcy to become one of the largest ever, second only to the collapse of Bear Sterns in 2008, when the $107 billion company revealed that assets had been inflated by about $11 billion.

When most people think of these scandals, they think of fraud, but fraud doesn't happen in a vacuum. It occurs when opportunity, financial pressure, and rationalization[18] converge. In these cases, abysmal to non-existent risk management created that opportunity. At Enron, the company hid billions in losses by creating partnerships with companies that it created. It had financial conflicts of interest with auditor Arthur Andersen, at the time one of the most prestigious accounting firms in the world and a member of the Big Five before it collapsed in the aftermath of the Enron scandal.

Much of that was due to the fact that Enron's board wasn't taking its responsibilities seriously. While the board defended itself by pointing out that Enron's management had hidden many of its questionable and fraudulent practices, a Senate Permanent Subcommittee investigation found there were "more than a dozen red flags" that were ignored. The committee said the board enabled the company's collapse "by allowing Enron to engage in high-risk accounting, inappropriate conflict of interest transactions, extensive undisclosed off-the-books activities, and excessive executive compensation. The Board witnessed numerous indications of questionable practices by Enron management over several years, but chose to ignore them to the detriment of Enron shareholders, employees, and business associates."[19]

What kind of risk-taking went on at Enron? Risk didn't even enter to the equation.

"Deals, especially in the finance division, were done at a rapid pace without much regard to whether they aligned with the strategic goals of the company or whether they complied with the company's risk management policies," reported Journal of Accountancy in 2002. "As one knowledgeable Enron employee put it: 'Good deal vs. bad deal? Didn't matter. If it had a positive net present value (NPV) it could get done. Sometimes positive NPV didn't even matter in the name of strategic significance.'"[20]

Most financial institution personnel look back on these scandals and think about how they led to the Sarbanes-Oxley Act of 2002, which increased regulatory burden with new internal control and attestation requirements. However, the scandals also brought heightened attention to risk management and the need for the ability to assess, identify, and mitigate risks across an institution. These scandals made it obvious COSO needed to provide guidance that went beyond operations, financial reporting, and compliance.

COSO AND MODERN-DAY ERM

Enter COSO's updated framework, which is designed to tackle ERM in a more complicated world. The newly revised framework introduces concepts such as:

Explicitly linking ERM with strategy and decision-making. An institution's mission, vision, and values don't exist in a vacuum. ERM is an essential tool for ensuring these three components are fully integrated into an institution's strategy and decisions. It explains why strategic risks and their alternatives should be addressed. It helps understand why strategies are chosen and how resources should be allocated.

Culture. As you'll soon read, culture plays a major role in the actions and performance of an institution. Unfortunately, there are too many institutions that don't embrace a risk management culture and the transparency and risk awareness it brings. COSO's updated framework demonstrates for the first time the role governance and culture play in a well-designed and executed ERM program, providing insights into how to ensure that employees at all levels make risk management part of their job description. It clarifies the board's role in developing an ERM culture and setting the institution's risk tolerance. The name of the game is accountability.

The relationship between risk management, performance, and value. Many institutions view ERM as a cost, when in reality, identifying, assessing, and mitigating risks saves an institution untold sums. Just consider the financial and reputational damage of every cyber breach, lawsuit, and enforcement action. COSO's framework helps demonstrate why ERM makes fiscal sense by creating stronger, more resilient institutions poised to take early action to exploit opportunities and defend against threats. ERM is not just about minimizing risk. It also understands how changes in risk impact decisions.

It pushes harder to break silos. The framework emphasizes that ERM connects to every department and function, allowing an institution to aggregate knowledge for a more complete picture. It helps an institution understand how truly interconnected its different areas are. This knowledge can increase efficiencies. It also helps an institution align its actions with its mission, values, and goals, helping ensure everyone has the same marching orders.

In the pages ahead, I'll make a case for why strategic planning and risk management must occur in tandem, reinforcing many aspects of COSO's ERM framework, which I urge you to examine closely.

The COSO framework emphasizes that ERM connects to every department and function, allowing an institution to aggregate knowledge for a more complete picture.

What Do the Financial Supervisory Agencies Have to Say About ERM?

While all financial regulatory agencies care about risk, they also recognize that different financial institutions have different needs.

NCUA

"Organizations can meet their specific needs with various tailored approaches that take into account their complexity, resources, and expertise. Credit unions that incorporate ERM into their infrastructure may resource the program internally, through paid consultants, or through a combination of outsourced and internal resources. NCUA does not view any approach as preferable, provided core principles, controls, and due diligence are properly established in the organization."[21]

NCUA goes on to say that there are several basic components that credit unions are likely to include: a risk culture, clear objectives, event identification, risk assessment, risk response, control activities, information and communication, and monitoring. It specifically highlights the COSO definition of ERM.

OCC

"No single risk management system works for all community banks. Each bank should develop a risk management system tailored to its specific needs and circumstances. The sophistication of the risk management system should be commensurate with the bank's size, complexity, and geographic diversity."[22]

However, all risk management systems need to identify, measure, and monitor risk, and set risk limits.

For example: "An important first step is selecting the right individual or committee to oversee the bank's ERM process. While a qualified individual independent from day-to-day business line management is preferred to oversee the ERM process, for a small bank this may not be practical or possible. In that case, consider senior level staff members who have a good understanding of the bank's operations across the various business lines. For example, a loan officer who does not have a complete understanding of operations or compliance requirements may not be fully capable of assessing all possible issues with a new deposit product. Placing that loan officer on a risk committee with staff members from other business lines, however, may result in an effective process and help ensure all relevant perspectives and potential risks are considered and addressed. As a check and balance, your bank may also consider engaging an outside consultant to periodically review the bank's ERM process independently."

Federal Reserve

When evaluating risk management, Fed examiners look for the following elements:

- Board and senior management oversight
- Policies, procedures, and limits
- Risk monitoring and management information systems
- Internal controls

However, the structure of the program is up to the bank. "An institution's risk management processes are expected to evolve in sophistication, commensurate with the institution's asset growth, complexity, and risk. At a larger or more complex organization, the institution should have more sophisticated risk management processes that address the full range of risks."[23]

The Fed goes on to give specific examples for each element, noting, for example, that while a large bank may benefit from an outside audit of internal controls, that may be overkill for a small institution. "In accordance with the Interagency Guidelines Establishing Standards for Safety and Soundness, a CBO [community banking organization] is expected, at a minimum, to have internal controls, information systems, and internal audit that are appropriate for the size of the institution and the nature, scope, and risk of its activities."

FDIC

In discussing each of the major risks banks face, the FDIC says that management should establish a risk management program that identifies, measures, monitors, and controls risks. Its intricacy and detail should be commensurate with the bank's size, complexity, and activities. Thus, the program should be tailored to the bank's needs and circumstances.

THE LIMITS OF FLEXIBILITY

While every risk management program should have the same goals of identifying, measuring, monitoring, and controlling risk, financial institutions have the freedom to structure these programs in a way that is most appropriate for their business, whether it's one single risk committee, a large risk department or a chief risk officer. In the parlance of the day, you do you.

But that doesn't mean that financial institutions can take a casual approach to risk management. Regulators have expectations for formal, documented programs that cover specific areas, including board oversight. They expect you to get from Point A to Point B and show them how you did it. They just give your institution the freedom to decide the best way to get there and hold it accountable if it fails to manage risk.

Citibank learned that lesson in late 2020 when the OCC hit the bank with a $400 million civil money penalty for data governance, risk management, and internal controls that resulted in unsafe or unsound practices when they were found to be insufficient for the bank's size.[24] The Federal Reserve also issued an enforcement action.

What went wrong?

The OCC says that Citi didn't implement or maintain an ERM and compliance risk management program commensurate with its size, complexity, and risk profile. Senior management oversight was inadequate to ensure timely, appropriate actions. Inadequate reporting hindered effective board oversight. The Fed found that risk management policies, procedures, and internal controls were hampered by insufficient staff training and expertise, undefined roles, and an inappropriate escalation framework.[25]

Both agencies required Citi to make corrections to its programs. The Fed required Citi to conduct a gap analysis to identify and remediate weaknesses and ensure it has timely, sufficient data on capital planning, liquidity, and compliance risk management to inform its ERM system and internal controls decisions. That includes how it will assess the accuracy and timeliness of the data. Until these issues are resolved, Citi will require OCC approval prior to significant acquisitions. The OCC can also require changes in senior management if the board doesn't meet progress deadlines.

Citi is not alone in its struggles. Lack of appropriate governance, oversight, and risk management systems and controls are the leading cause of enforcement actions, according to the OCC.[26] The most common areas for risk management enforcement actions include compliance or operational failures. When it comes to matters requiring attention (MRA), the top two concerns are operational risk (40 percent) and compliance risk (24 percent) followed by credit risk (23 percent).

Capitol One's risk management practices were criticized as part of a 2020 OCC consent order that came with an $80 million fine after a data breach exposed the data of 100 million Americans and 6 million Canadians, including names, addresses, zip codes/postal codes, phone numbers, email addresses, birthdates, income, credit scores, and payment history.[27] The breach went on for three months before the bank was tipped off by an anonymous email.

The OCC blamed the breach on Capital One's failure to establish effective risk management processes and address operational risk management weaknesses. The company "failed to establish effective risk assessment processes" before moving IT operations to the cloud. It "failed to establish appropriate risk management" for operating in the cloud. This includes designing and implementing internal controls for network security and data loss prevention. Capital One's internal auditors failed to recognize numerous control weaknesses and gaps. Those they did find were not effectively reported. When presented with internal audit's concerns, the board didn't effectively hold management accountable.

Data breaches are a common result of poor risk management. The New York Department of Financial Services (NYDFS) filed its first enforcement action under its cybersecurity regulations in 2020, charging

Nebraska-based First American Title Company with exposing more than 850 million documents containing private customer data over at least four years between 2014 and May 2019. Not only did the title company fail to perform a risk assessment of its computer program, NYDFS said, but it also misclassified the level of risk the security flaw presented. The vulnerability was labeled as "medium severity" even though it had the potential to expose sensitive customer data.[28] The title company didn't follow its own policies, keep up with findings, hold anyone accountable for remediation, listen to its internal cyber experts or encrypt data. It had poor controls and relied on manual processes that failed.

Effective enterprise risk management could have prevented each of these enforcement actions. Instead, these companies ended up having to invest in large-scale improvements to their ERM programs and pay substantial fines, which makes their mistakes documented and publicized. It would have been much smarter, not to mention cheaper, to have appropriate ERM in place from the beginning and use a risk management lens to examine activities before diving in.

THE THREE LINES OF DEFENSE

COSO isn't the only organization to emphasize the role of the board and management in its update to risk management models. In 2020, the Institute of Internal Auditors updated its Three Lines of Defense,[29] a widely adopted model that helps identify and define risk management roles and responsibilities. While the old model focused on the three lines of defense (operational management, risk and compliance management, and internal audit) and the avoidance of risk, the updated Three Lines Model is more focused on governance, collaboration, and the role of risk management in creating and protecting value.

The IIA's **Three Lines Model**

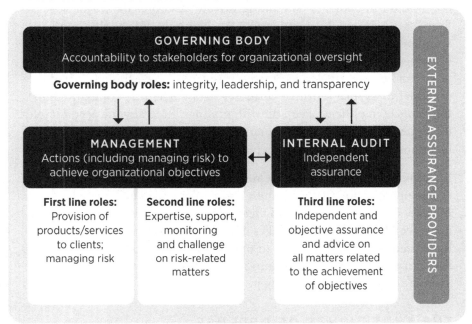

Working together under the guidance of management and the board, the three lines implement and oversee activities and controls that ensure the organization is working towards its strategic objectives while remaining within its risk tolerance.

- **First Line.** The first line is operational management. These are the managers and process owners responsible for the institution's day-to-day activities. They create and apply internal controls to respond to risks in their area of operations, whether its sales or back-office operations.

- **Second Line.** The second line provides assistance with managing risk, including supporting and challenging the first line. In financial institutions, the second line is made up of compliance and risk management, which are responsible for creating and executing the policies, procedures, and systems that oversee and guide the first line of defense. Roles may include monitoring, advice, guidance, testing, analyzing, and reporting on risk management matters.

Risk management is responsible for assessing the risk of all business activities. If a business activity doesn't fall within the FI's risk tolerance, internal controls need to be added or adjusted—or the activity may need to be discontinued. Risk management also identifies high-risk areas that require increased scrutiny in the form of testing and monitoring to ensure the first line is working as intended to comply with rules and regulations.

Compliance is responsible for identifying applicable laws and regulations, interpreting them, and then developing and enforcing policies and procedures to support them through a compliance management system (CMS). It should work hand-in-hand with risk management to ensure risk assessments are thorough and up to date.

Risk management and compliance are also responsible, in most institutions, for fostering relations between the first and third line of defense and providing some reporting to the board and senior management. While different FIs will divvy up these responsibilities in different ways and to different areas, the bottom line is that risk management and compliance play an essential role in ensuring effective risk management.

- **The Third Line.** The third line of defense is internal audit. Internal audit objectively and independently evaluates risks and controls and provides advice on their efficacy. They are also responsible for reporting on risk to the board, senior management, and other stakeholders. A good audit program allows an FI one last chance to uncover internal flaws that are hindering compliance.

The third line of defense helps identify and uncover problems and helps ensure findings are addressed promptly and consistently. Auditing provides no value if you don't do anything with the information. Being able to visualize and remediate problems is an essential step in assuring that risks are appropriately mitigated and the organization is ready for external regulatory exams and reviews. It makes sure that an FI identifies and corrects problems itself, rather than waiting for an examiner to uncover an issue.

The third line should focus its efforts on the areas where risk exposure is the greatest.

TWO OUT OF THREE IS BAD

With apologies to Meat Loaf and his 1977 power ballad, having just two of the three lines of defense isn't good.

If only one line of defense is working well, it can present risks to the other lines as well as the institution. It's a lesson JP Morgan learned the hard way in November 2020 when the OCC hit the bank with a $250 million civil money penalty for failing to maintain adequate internal controls and internal audit over its fiduciary business—an unsafe and unsound practice.[30]

What exactly went wrong? While the enforcement action was short on details, we do know that for several years the bank maintained a weak management and control framework for its fiduciary activities, according to the OCC. That includes: an insufficient audit program; inadequate internal controls; inefficient risk management practices; and an insufficient framework for avoiding conflicts of interest.

The OCC says these audit and risk management deficiencies violated 12 CFR 9.9, which requires a suitable audit over all significant fiduciary activities.

A fiduciary relationship requires an institution to act for the benefit of the customer when acting on the customer's behalf. The fact that the enforcement action specifically mentions "an insufficient framework for avoiding conflicts of interest" suggests that JP Morgan might not have been doing enough to ensure the actions of its employees were for the benefit of its clients—and not the benefit of the bank or its bankers.

It's something the bank should have been actively policing, especially from a risk management perspective. Fiduciary activities are a source of significant risk. There's compliance risk, which can cost the bank both financially with fines and strategically if it causes regulators to limit acquisitions or other expansions. There's operational and transaction risk. There's also substantial reputation risk. Consumers remember headlines that suggest a financial institution can't be trusted to take care of their assets.

There's also the fact that JP Morgan has gotten in trouble for similar problems in the past. In 2015 the bank had to pay over $300 million to the SEC and U.S. Commodities Future Trading Corporation and admit it failed to disclose conflicts of interest to clients between 2008 and 2013. (JP Morgan referred clients to invest in the firm's own, higher-priced proprietary investment products without proper disclosures). Regulatory agencies don't like repeat findings.

The bank should have interpreted that fine as a wake-up call to ensure its wealth management program had internal controls in place to proactively monitor and remediate potential conflicts of interest. Now the OCC says the bank has remediated the deficiencies that led to the OCC's action.

Looking at the JP Morgan enforcement action, it's possible that all three lines of defense failed.

1. **First line of defense:** Conflicts of interest that benefit an institution's bottom line don't just happen. Someone makes that choice. Were employees incentivized to make choices that resulted in conflicts of interest? Was this incentive intended or unintended? Did their managers know they were making this decision and choosing to ignore it or were they ignorant? There's plenty of potential blame to go around. If the first line of defense was functioning, employees would be following policies and procedures. That leads us to the role of the second line of defense.

2. **Second line of defense:** Risk management and compliance. Risk management should have recognized that its fiduciary business was high-risk and required an increased level of risk management, mitigation, and monitoring. There should have been policies and procedures in place to prevent and detect conflicts of interest. Either these policies didn't exist or weren't effective. The framework for managing this risk was insufficient and internal controls were inadequate.

3. **Third line of defense:** Audit. The audit program at JP Morgan was insufficient and failed to recognize the bank had inadequate internal controls. It's hard to follow up on the effectiveness of controls that aren't appropriate in the first place, but a good audit program should have noticed controls weren't doing their job.

Three strong lines of defense led by a governing body that promotes risk management and creates accountability—as we'll learn later in the chapter on governance.

A financial institution must always be looking forward, ahead, and at the present when it comes to risk management. COSO and the Three Lines Model help make that possible.

CHAPTER FOUR

IDENTIFYING RISK

When the vendor has a problem, the financial institution makes the news.

R isk is unavoidable, but it's not unknowable. While every financial institution faces its share of surprises and setbacks, many of the risks of doing business can be identified and mitigated with the help of thoughtful risk assessments.

The key word here is *thoughtful.* When conducted properly, risk assessments are highly effective tools that help ensure risk is aligned with an institution's strategic objectives. A well-executed risk assessment digs into real-world risks and the specific controls an institution uses to mitigate their impact, allowing the board and management to make better, more insightful decisions. From big picture ideas to specific areas of concern, a good risk assessment looks at the good and bad in every situation to provide a thorough understanding of threats and opportunities.

The applications are broad. From observations on potential new products and services to setting budget priorities to pointing out areas in need of compliance reviews, a smart risk assessment gives the board and management a valuable viewpoint. It can uncover weaknesses in controls or risk scenarios when disaster planning, shed light on policies that act as controls, assess the ongoing effectiveness of automated controls, aid with vendor selection and ongoing vendor management, and suggest new controls or improvements to existing ones.

THE RISK MANAGEMENT LIFECYCLE

Too many financial institutions view risk assessments as one-time events. They gather information to help set strategy and make operational decisions. Once they identify risks that could derail strategic objectives, the assessment is forgotten.

That's a mistake. A risk assessment isn't an event or an item that can be completed once and crossed off a checklist. As the world both outside and inside an institution evolves, so does the institution's risk exposure. An institution must actively engage in risk management, assessing risk and making adjustments to ensure its risk exposure is aligned with its goals. This active engagement is needed to determine if those goals are even still appropriate.

A risk assessment is just the first step in the risk assessment lifecycle, a multi-step process that includes assessing risk, evaluating the control environment, communicating the results, and remediating any failed or ineffective controls. On its own, a risk assessment is a valuable tool, but it's just the beginning. Without follow up to ensure that the information it contains is used, evaluated, and updated, it quickly becomes a dead document.

The diagram on page 51 depicts the risk management lifecycle. It begins with the risk assessment. Once the risk assessment is completed, its insights are used to drive the scope and frequency of internal control testing. Controls that are critical to mitigating significant risks should be tested more often than less important controls or those that mitigate less substantial risks.

Internal control testing involves reviewing the effectiveness of controls. Testers select a sampling of documents and transactions to evaluate how effective they are. This can include whether policies and procedures are followed, the completeness of documents, and the accuracy of data. Auditors can be positioned as testers due to their core competencies in this area. This adds value to the entire ERM program, while gaining synergies by more closely aligning back-office processes.

Recommendations from internal controls testing are then passed on to management, who reviews the findings and makes decisions to accept, defer, or reject the recommendations. This often involves updating risks and controls, beginning the cycle begins anew.

Risk Management Lifecycle

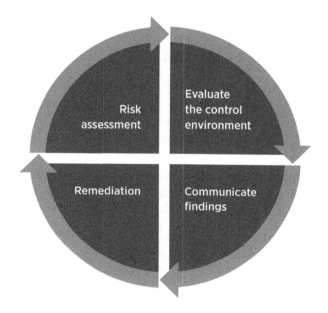

Initially the lifecycle was developed as an annual exercise, but realistically it has been extended to roughly once in-between examinations. The FFIEC IT Exam Handbook—Audit guidance suggests that the audit frequency of any particular control is directly related to the inherent risk value that the control remediates.

THE RISK ASSESSMENT PROCESS

Now that we understand where the risk assessment fits into the overall risk management lifecycle, let's delve into the specifics. Before starting a risk assessment, it's essential to bring together all the actors and agree upon some basic ground rules. These include:

1. Establishing the context
2. Risk identification
3. Risk analysis & evaluation
4. Risk treatment
5. Monitoring and review
6. Communication

Let's start at the beginning with the first two items, establishing the context and risk identification. We'll go in-depth on the rest of the lifecycle in subsequent chapters.

ESTABLISHING THE CONTEXT

An accurate risk assessment is only possible when the whole team knows what is being assessed and how it works. The institution needs to decide on the specific business activity, process, or project that is going to be covered to determine the scope or context of the risk assessment. This can be a broad category like operational risk or credit risk or a specific department, product, or service like compliance, credit cards, or mobile banking. A risk assessment will periodically assess each business line, product, service, or system against each risk category to identify key risk drivers.

Once the area is selected, the institution should conduct an extensive review of background information. Business plans are an excellent source of information, helping the team to understand management's objectives.

When considering the business model, there are four areas that need to be discussed: clients, value, capabilities, and financial structure.

Clients. Think about the institution's core clients and business segments. What are the key needs the institution fulfills for these clients? It can be anything from relationships or branch locations to industry-specific products and services. How strong are these client relationships and how hard is it for clients to leave? Are they locked into agreements?

Value. Value can be defined with a simple question: why choose us? This involves understanding what your institution does to meet needs and create value for clients.

Capabilities. Assessing the institution's capabilities requires looking internally at resources. What technology does the institution need to provide service to clients? Does it rely on a strategic partner to deliver products and services? What processes are needed to deliver value to clients? What internal team members are needed to deliver value?

Financial structure. Identifying key clients and market segments helps an institution know who or what generates revenue. In the case of COVID-19, an institution that serves the hospitality industry had very different financial results than one that provides professional services such as health care. It's also necessary to identify the expenses involved in providing value to these clients.

It's also important to understand management's risk tolerances and thresholds. Depending on the institution, several sources of background info may be available. Review the results of any strengths, weaknesses, opportunities, and threats (SWOT) or political, environmental, social, and technological (PEST) analysis as well as ratio analysis. Determine if there have been any changes to applicable guidance since the last assessment. Conducting and documenting this analysis provides a foundation for strengthening an institution's business position and identifying risk. This can be done at the enterprise level or on a department-by-department basis.

This information will help ensure that assessors aren't working in a vacuum. The more they know about how an area functions and where things can go wrong, the more equipped they'll be to address those risks. It also ensures they are focused on a particularly defined risk area.

RISK IDENTIFICATION

Every institution faces a host of risks and opportunities. Some of them are obvious while others are harder to sleuth out. The most common categories of risk include operational, transaction, compliance, credit, strategic, reputation, third-party, cyber, and concentration risk. An effective risk assessment probes deeply into these broad categories and explores risk at a granular level to understand new, emerging, and changing risks.

The COSO framework recommends identifying "risks that are likely to disrupt operations and affect the reasonable expectation of achieving strategy and business objectives."

Risks can come from both inside and outside an institution. A change in strategy, a new business line, a new vendor, or a new market can all present new risks. For instance, if the institution chooses to transition from physical servers to a cloud environment, it introduces a variety of potential risks.

These include:

- **Third-party risk.** How strong is the vendor? Is it likely to go under?
- **Fourth-party risk.** If the vendor relies on subcontractors, how well are they vetted?
- **Cyber.** How secure are the new servers?
- **Operational.** In what scenarios could this technology fail?
- **Transaction.** What are the business continuity planning issues that must be addressed?
- **Strategic risk.** Is there a chance this won't support the institution's long-term goals?
- **Reputational.** What could go wrong with this vendor that could impact the institution's reputation?
- **Compliance.** Regulators see no difference between an institution and its vendors when it comes to compliance. Does the vendor follow all applicable laws, regulations, and institutional procedures?

External factors that can introduce risk include regulatory changes, technological advances, new competition, evolving consumer demands, and economic conditions.

That's exactly what happened when the COVID-19 pandemic began spreading across the U.S. in early 2020. As news about the emerging virus grew from bad to worse and many communities moved into lockdown, financial institutions had to reevaluate and reinvent their approach to banking when the branch channel became unavailable.

A good COVID-19 response plan did more than preserve value. It identified risk. It created value by evaluating and modifying the business model to improve resilience and decrease risk. It provided a structure for navigating risks after they were identified. It identified risk.

Then they had to consider how COVID-19 could affect the institution, including how it could change identified clients' needs, core clients' supply chains, and employee needs. It was also necessary to think about COVID-19's impact on branches, the ability of loan officers to meet with new clients or attract opportunities, and how the timing of these issues effects the FI's business model. For example, institutions that predicted mortgage demand would increase due to the change in interest rates and planned strategically for increased volume were well-positioned to profit from the 2020 mortgage boom, which saw record mortgage originations of nearly $4 billion.

Risks related to COVID-19 included employee absenteeism, spread of the virus in branches, health confidentiality, teleworking, increased cyberattacks, limited opportunities to interact with consumers, regulatory change and guidance, loan losses and charge-offs, reduced profitability, and critical vendor failure, among others.

Another external risk area to consider is the emerging fintech industry. Fintech is a broad term. On the one hand, it includes a huge swath of nonbank payment and technology providers that often compete directly with banks and credit unions while piggybacking on existing payments networks. This ranges from lenders, such as Square and Lending Club, to person-to-person payment providers, like Venmo and PayPal, and wealth management and robo-advising, like Wealthfront and Betterment. On the other side are the third-party vendors and partners that enable regulated financial institutions to compete. This includes everyone from mobile banking and digital wallet providers to core vendors. It's a huge umbrella.

While fintech offers opportunities for partnering with third parties to provide customers new products and services, it also introduces a new source of competition in lending. Fintechs originated 38 percent of unsecured consumer loans balances in 2018, compared to just 5 percent in 2013, according to a TransUnion study.[31] During the same period bank-originated balances declined from 40 percent to 28 percent while credit unions dropped from 31 percent to 21 percent. While many fintechs aim for lower-tier credit customers, which result in higher delinquencies, they also have higher returns than banks and credit unions.

This evolving competition presents a host of threats and opportunities that can be identified by examining potential risks. Do changing customer expectations impact how customers view the bank's technology? Do customers prefer elements of the fintech's offerings over the institution's own? Are the bank's existing product offerings still relevant and competitive? Are the fintechs coming after the institution's best customers? Is there a way to leverage fintechs to keep pace? Is trying to compete with fintechs worth the financial investment?

The answers to these questions will vary from institution to institution. A small, rural community bank mainly involved in agricultural lending may decide its customers are unlikely to jump ship to an online lender or aren't asking for mobile banking, and so may decide the return won't justify the investment in new technologies. It might not feel that fintechs present a risk to its model. A growing institution courting Gen Z may see more competition from fintech providers and view them as a greater risk to their business model.

It's also important to remember that risk doesn't fit neatly into a singular box. As the example of adopting the cloud shows, one risk can have an impact on a variety of strategies, objectives, departments, business lines, levels of management, locations, products, services, policies, and procedures.

Checklists, roundtable discussions, and existing management reports and data can be great sources for brainstorming potential risks. Use annual events like budgeting, performance reviews, and strategic planning sessions to talk about new, emerging, and changing risks. Go beyond the obvious, easy-to-spot risks. This takes time and creativity, it but will result in a vastly improved risk assessment.

Use this time to think globally about the broad range of things that can go wrong at institutions of a similar size and type. A mid-sized community institution shouldn't necessarily compare itself to a multi-national organization, nor should it rely exclusively only on its own experiences. The guidance from federal regulators and the Federal Financial Institutions Examination Council (FFIEC) can help guide this process.

POTENTIAL RISKS: A DEEP DIVE

When it comes to risk, financial institutions are acutely aware of the risks of lending. They know how a borrower's history, loan-to-value ratio, debt service coverage ratio, collateral, covenants, and loan structure impact the potential risk a specific borrower presents.

An institution has to consider its own financial and business conditions as well, including its loan to value ratio, lending concentration risk, and strategic objectives. It needs to have the right loan officers in the right place and have the underwriting technology and back-office support necessary to promptly close and service loans.

There's also lending compliance to consider, particularly when it comes to fair lending and ensuring equal treatment of customers, a common source of enforcement and legal action. This includes ensuring that services are marketed in all areas, similar customers receive similar pricing and products, and all underwriting decisions are objective while preventing redlining. In just 2020 alone, Wells Fargo settled a $20 million suit with the city of Philadelphia for steering minorities into higher-cost, higher-risk mortgage loans. USAA's Community Reinvestment Act (CRA) rating was downgraded to "Needs to improve" after the OCC uncovered evidence of discriminatory and illegal credit practices, and the CFPB sued a Chicago mortgage company for redlining. Compliance with laws and regulations also impacts how loans are marketed and serviced. If the institution relies on third parties to aid in the process, that adds another layer of risk.

It's clear that lending risk is a lot more involved than simple dollars and cents. It ties into the whole enterprise, touching compliance, IT, human resources, operations, and finance, among others. To look at just one of these elements is to leave out critical information that helps an institution understand the totality of its risk exposure.

Yet not every risk is as obvious as those involved in lending. Let's highlight three commons risk areas to understand their potential impact on an institution: third-party vendor risk, human capital risk, and political risk.

THIRD-PARTY VENDOR RISK

Staying relevant means relying on hundreds of vendors who provide products and services. Unfortunately, these third-party relationships can create significant risk. Regulators view actions taken by third-party vendors on behalf of a financial institution no differently than the actual actions of the institution. That means just about anything that can go wrong with an institution can go wrong with its vendor, making it essential to risk assess vendors, particularly those who play a significant role at the institution. According to the FDIC,[32] areas to consider include:

- **Financial condition:** Audited financial statements, filings, annual reports, litigation, and how the contract would impact the vendor's financial condition.

- **Experience:** Does the company have the experience and capacity to do the job? Will it need to expand to accommodate the FI? What other business activities is it engaged in? Is it knowledgeable about consumer protection laws and regulations? What are the qualifications of its principals?
- **Business approach:** "Strategies and goals, including service philosophies, quality initiatives, efficiency improvements, and employment policies." Also inquire about use of subcontractors and vendor and institution management responsibilities.
- **Internal controls:** What kind of internal controls, systems, and data security and privacy protections does the vendor have? Does it have audit coverage? What are its business resumption, continuity, and contingency plans? How strong are its management information systems? Does it have insurance coverage? What are its underwriting criteria?
- **Marketing:** How will the vendor use the institution's name on materials and websites?

Many of the most high-profile cybersecurity breaches in recent years have been due to third-party vendors. In 2020, SolarWinds' Orion software, a platform designed to monitor and manage IT security and used by thousands of U.S. companies and government branches, was breached by Russian state-backed hackers. By inserting malicious code into software updates, hackers opened a backdoor into the software, which allowed them to spy on internal emails at the U.S. Treasury and Commerce departments and access Microsoft's source code among other yet-to-be-discovered breaches. The hack went undetected for months.

While the SolarWinds hack is especially noteworthy for its size, it's not shocking when you consider how often breaches occur. A study released by the Ponemon Institute in 2018 found that 59 percent of respondents in the U.S. and U.K. report that a third party caused a data breach.[33] That includes the 42 percent of organizations that experienced a vendor-related data breach in the past 12 months. Another 22 percent didn't even know if they'd been exposed by a third-party data breach. A 2013 study by digital security company Trustwave noted that third parties were responsible for 63 percent of breaches.

In other breaches, in 2017 a hacker pirated the fifth season of hit Netflix show *Orange is the New Black,* and leaked the show online more than a month before it was scheduled to hit the Netflix platform after the company refused to pay ransom. The leak is believed to have stemmed from Larson Studios, the company that handles post-production audio for the "dramedy," *Variety* reported. Data from at least 6 million Verizon Wireless users was leaked online the same year, including phone numbers, names, and PIN numbers to access accounts. NICE Systems, a vendor Verizon Wireless was using to manage customer service phone calls, set an Amazon S3 storage server to public instead of private, CNN reported.[34] Anyone with a link could access data on the server until the problem was fixed, which was more than a week after it was discovered. Meanwhile, some of the most high-end hotel chains in the country, including Four Seasons, Trump Hotels, Hard Rock Hotels & Casinos, and Loews Hotels faced a similar issue when guest data, including credit card and contract information, was exposed for about eight months in 2017. The common thread the hotels shared: Sabre Hospitality Solutions SynXis Central Reservation system. More than 36,000 properties use the system.

IT'S A PROBLEM THAT IMPACTS FINANCIAL INSTITUTIONS, TOO.

Routine security monitoring detected unauthorized access to Corporations Services Company's (CSC) network and systems in April 2018. The company, which serves over 3,000 financial institutions, said that a database with client information containing at least 5,600 individuals' names, Social Security numbers, or credit/debit card information was stolen. More than 20,000 ScottTrade Bank customers' sensitive information was exposed in 2017 when third-party vendor Genpact uploaded data to the cloud without enabling all the necessary security protocols.

Then there's the Texas credit union that used a third-party vendor for data analytic services. The vendor was a victim of a ransomware attack that resulted in thousands of member files being compromised, including Social Security numbers. As a result, the credit union had to notify thousands of members of the data breach and explain the issue with their vendor management program. In addition, the credit union had to provide each member identification repair and monitoring services at the cost of hundreds of thousands of dollars.

Oversight of vendor cybersecurity is a common problem at financial institutions, according to the FDIC's Office of Inspector General's evaluation Technology Service Provider Contracts with FDIC-Supervised Institutions, which focuses on business continuity planning and cyber incident response. The evaluation found that "often FI contracts with TSPs are dated and do not reflect FDIC and FFIEC efforts to strengthen cybersecurity."[35] Many vendor contracts don't address vendor responsibility for assessing and responding to incidents; determining the potential effect on the institution or its customers; or reporting and notifying authorities.

Beyond Gramm-Leach-Bliley and customer privacy regulations, a vendor can pose other compliance risks, failing to follow other federal laws or regulations. One Missouri bank was forced to pay consumers $5 million in restitution after a third-party vendor deceptively marketed balance transfer credit cards, violating section 5 of the Federal Trade Commission (FTC) Act according to a Federal Reserve consent order.[36] The bank used a third-party independent service organizations (ISOs) to market a variety of balance transfer credit cards to consumers. The ISOs bought debt and then marketed credit cards through the bank. In exchange for transferring their debt to the new card, the ISO would forgive a portion of the debt. The problem is that the ISOs didn't always deliver on the promises, according to the consent order. One card marketed through an ISO to consumers with charged-off debt didn't accurately disclose that participating in the program could restart the statute of limitation on debt, affecting about 8,000 consumers with charged-off debts outside of the statute of limitations.

Another Missouri bank faced a $1.5 million civil money penalty as part of an OCC enforcement action[37] after allegedly violating Section 5 of the FTC Act by incorrectly billing customers who purchased an identity theft product. The OCC blamed it on "deficient vendor management practices" and required the bank to improve its vendor management processes.

In 2016 the Consumer Financial Protection Bureau (CFPB) hit Santander Bank with a $10 million fine[38] for illegal overdraft practices, even though not a single one of its employees violated Reg E. Its vendor did. Reg E's Opt-In Rule requires that financial institutions get consumers' opt-in consent before charging overdraft fees. The vendor ignored those rules and used deceptive practices to enroll customers in the bank's overdraft program without consent and misrepresented the cost of the service, according to the CFPB.

Some banks have been falling short when it comes to change management. Numerous institutions had issues with third-party vendors that weren't ready for changes to the integrated mortgage disclosures under the Truth in Lending Act (TILA) and Real Estate Settlement Procedures Act (RESPA) in 2014.[39] Strong due diligence processes and ongoing monitoring for critical third-party vendors is a must, the agency notes, citing TILA-RESPA and the Military Lending Act (MLA) as examples where institutions rely on vendors for loan application processing, disclosures, underwriting, and closing.

Vendors must be financially stable, reliable, and have strong disaster recovery plans. Many pages of regulatory guidance have been written to protect institutions, yet a recent analysis conducted by the FDIC's Office of Inspector General finds that just half of vendor contracts it reviewed "explicitly included business continuity provisions."[40]

When a financial institution outsources to a third-party vendor, it's responsible for ensuring the vendor has a business continuity plan to promptly recover and resume operations in the event of a disruption. These plans include a business impact analysis, a risk assessment, risk management, and risk monitoring and testing, the OIG notes.

This can only be done effectively when the institution can "coordinate its risk management processes with the service provider's operations and plans." Unfortunately, most contracts don't include the level of detail necessary to make this happen. In fact, nearly half don't even require vendors to have a business continuity plan. That's because institutions aren't identifying this risk and then taking action to mitigate it.[41]

OPERATIONAL RISK

Then there's operational risk. Vendor consolidation is contributing to elevated levels of operational risk for banks.[42] As the ecosystem of vendors shrinks, FIs have fewer options and more of them are relying on the same third-party vendors to support critical operations. This includes core processors, merchant card processing, denial of service mitigation, and trust accounting systems. The result of vendor concentration is systemic risk, or the risk that an entire financial system or entire market could collapse. Should a major third-party provider encounter difficulty, it could interrupt operations for a large portion of the industry, making oversight essential.

It's also critical to consider fourth-party risk, or the risk posed by a vendor's subcontractors and partners. It's not always enough to conduct due diligence on a third-party vendor. That vendor may rely on critical vendors of its own whose performance could impact the institution's operations.

In the race to remain competitive, nearly 4,000[43] banks and credit unions have signed on to Apple Pay, probably hoping that some of Apple's cool will rub off on them. But how high is the price of that affiliation? I'm not talking about Apple's cost per transaction fees. I'm talking about the potential risks to client data.

In the event of fraud, institutions may not be able to look to Apple for restitution. This may seem ridiculous. Apple owns the operating environment and controls the app store. But it doesn't own the responsibility.

People will try to tell you this isn't a big deal. Apple's security is amazing, they say. Apple uses cutting-edge technology, including near field communications (NFC) and EMV tokenization standards. Neither Apple, the device, nor retailers store actual credit card data so there is nothing for hackers to steal. The device must be used with the finger-print reader, facial scanner, or the phone's passcode for NFC to work.

But never say never. Hackers always find a way, and some already have by making individual phones targets.

When it comes to cybersecurity risk, never say never.
Hackers always find a way.

The scam is simple. Fraudsters enter stolen credit cards into Apple Pay accounts and start shopping.[44] Apple doesn't require issuers to do much to verify the authenticity of accounts. This security matter is left to the issuer and those standards vary greatly from institution to institution. Even those that require a phone call often ask questions that can be answered with a Google search (a process called social engineering).[45] Some cite fraud as high as six percent, according to *2015 Bank Info Security* report.[46] A *Forbes* article cited a source who suggested that this process is easier on Apple Pay than on Google and Samsung's platforms because Apple doesn't use "rate limiting" to limit the number times a person (or computer) can guess the three-digit CVV code. But that's not really Apple's problem, is it? They bear no financial responsibility for the fraud.

That's just the threat we know about. There are other potential issues as the CNBC[47] report points out. It suggests other threats including:

- **Third-party apps.** Most people think of Apple Pay as a point-of-sale (POS) tool where consumers use their iPhones and Apple Watches for NFC transactions. Yet Apple Pay can also be used within apps for card-not-present transactions. Retailers can design apps to accept Apple Pay—and the financial institution has no control over how secure these mobile payment apps are. There could be security flaws for hackers to exploit, and Apple is not responsible for them.
- **Touch ID and Face ID.** Apple's fingerprint reader and facial scanner have been hacked in experiments.

Who knows what else hackers will think of? It's not entirely an exercise in speculation. Just think of the iCloud scandal back in 2014, when celebrities' phones were hacked, and personal photos and other information was stolen. There could be an unknown flaw in the NFC system. And then there are the consumers who "jailbreak" their phones, changing the iOS, Apple's operating system. Who knows what kind of vulnerabilities they introduce? These are all risks that must be taken into account before adopting a strategy.

Ignoring vendor risk is a huge oversight, and not just because of the potential risks discussed above. Vendor management is also a regulatory hot-button issue with all the major financial regulators providing specific guidance on third-party vendor management. That means managing third-party vendor relationships is also a compliance risk.

HUMAN CAPITAL RISK

The human resources department can play a significant role in helping an institution achieve its business objectives by aligning in-house talent with strategic plans. This can only be accomplished when the institution is aware of the potential risks human capital presents in terms of both threats and opportunities.

Every institution needs talent to achieve its goals. Not having enough talent or lacking the right talent can pose serious operational risks. An institution that can't attract and retain strong talent with the right skills is at a competitive disadvantage and faces the possibility of failing to meet strategic goals. This is especially true when it comes to succession planning and growing future leaders.

The changing workplace and technological environment can present risk and opportunities, from permitting employees to work remotely to the potential for an employee to post something to social media that could negatively impact the institution. Employees suffering from low morale may perform poorly while bad hires can be worse than not having enough staff. High turnover can create a lack of institutional knowledge and stability. There are also compliance risks, such as ensuring that hiring practices are compliant with state and federal law, including Title VII of the Civil Rights Act of 1964, which prohibits employment discrimination based on race, color, religion, sex, or national origin.

Human capital risk was front and center during the COVID-19 pandemic. Financial institutions found themselves managing a remote workforce for the first time. Many employees worked on their personal devices using their home Wi-Fi connection, creating considerable IT security risk. Other prominent work-from-home risks included control access, privacy, technology, bandwidth, and employee performance, among others.

The risk of insufficient and improper employee training resources resulting in noncompliance with laws, regulations, policies, procedures, and institutional rules is another concern. Consider the case of Thomas E. Haider, the former chief compliance officer of MoneyGram International, who was fined $250,000 by the Financial Crimes Enforcement Network (FinCEN) and banned from serving in a compliance function for any money transmitter for the following three years. FinCEN said he created "an environment where fraud and money laundering thrived and dirty money rampaged."[48]

As part of the settlement, FinCEN says Haider accepted responsibility for failing to close outlets involved in consumer fraud schemes; not developing policies for closing outlets at a high risk of fraud; and a poorly designed anti-money laundering (AML) program that didn't share fraud information with internal analysts who filed SAR reports. Haider's failure to control fraud resulted in thousands of consumers, especially the elderly, getting tricked into sending money at participating MoneyGram outlets because they thought they were paying taxes on lottery winnings and prizes or upfront fees for a loan when they were really being scammed, FinCEN said.

As FinCEN put it, "His inaction led to thousands of innocent individuals being duped out of millions of dollars through fraud schemes that funneled, and sometimes laundered, their illicit profits through Money-Gram's money transmission network."

There can also be problems on an individual level when people don't follow appropriate policies and procedures. Wells Fargo, which keeps finding itself the subject of bad newspaper headlines, found itself in the news again when a teller in a Washington, D.C., stole over $185,000 from a homeless customer.[49] The customer was a street vendor who unsuccessfully attempted to deposit thousands in cash into a dormant account. The teller checked the customer's balance, saw he had a lot of cash and plotted to steal it. He opened a new account for the customer without telling him and transferred the cash there. The teller then opened an ATM card and used it 144 times over two years to withdraw a total of $185,440 to pay down debt and go on several Caribbean vacations. The customer knew nothing of the theft since he didn't receive bank statements, didn't use email, and didn't have a computer.

While in a normal environment this wouldn't have been more than a local story, the teller's actions made national news because it fit a publicly perceived pattern of Wells Fargo's malfeasance.

POLITICAL RISK

Due to their strict regulation, banks and credit unions tend to view political risk from a regulatory standpoint. The outlook of elected officials at the local, state, and national level influences the laws that are passed, the rules that are implemented, and the enforcement of regulations. The industry tends to generalize that certain candidates and parties are good for deregulation, while others are more likely to increase regulation.

There is risk in relying too heavily on these assumptions. While the industry heralded the arrival of President Donald Trump's administration as a time for deregulation, believing that his stated opposition to heavy regulation would yield significant regulatory relief, those changes were slow to materialize. Even when one party holds the House of Representatives, the Senate, and the presidency, the passage and implementation of high-priority legislation can be bogged down by infighting and other distractions. Consider the first two years of Barack Obama's presidency. Despite holding both the House and the Senate for two years, it took years for the Democrats to pass healthcare reform and that barely made it through because of disagreements over the details.

While pro-regulatory relief candidates and elected officials inspire hope for regulatory relief, these are not promises that can be taken to the bank. It's dangerous to assume that an institution will be able to spend less on compliance or put less emphasis on certain regulations until actual rules have been passed. Even proposals should not be counted on when making projections about the future, as they often change between the time they are first published for comment and their final form. Sometimes these changes can be beneficial, but this is not always the case.

Another political risk to beware of is donating to a candidate's political action committee or PAC. These are funds used by candidates and causes to run their campaigns, including paying staffers, buying ads, renting space for rallies, etc. While corporations cannot make donations directly to political candidates, individuals can donate up to a limit. Many financial institutions encourage board members and management to support candidates favorable to their business agenda. U.S. law requires candidates to publicly disclose the name of any individual who donates more than $200 to their campaign. That means the public can easily find out if an institution's leadership is supporting a specific candidate. While this typically isn't a huge risk, if a candidate turns out to be controversial or highly unpopular with customers, it could create public relations issues if the institution is strongly linked with that candidate. On the other hand, failing to support a candidate may be a lost opportunity to strengthen an important relationship.

It's not just individual candidates that can create political risk. There is also the risk of supporting or doing business with an organization that's controversial or becomes increasingly controversial. Consider the case of First National Bank of Omaha, the nation's largest privately-owned bank. For years, the bank offered a co-branded Visa credit card with the National Rifle Association (NRA), but in 2018 the bank found itself in an awkward position after a gunman killed 17 people and injured 15 at Marjory Stoneman Douglas High School in Parkland, Fla., igniting a national conversation about gun control. The NRA's vocal support for the Second Amendment drew heated criticism from gun control advocates, and many customers used social media to let First National Bank know that they were uncomfortable banking with an institution that worked with the NRA. One such group was Nebraskans Against Gun Violence, which said it would plan a public protest, drawing more attention to the issue. The website ThinkProgress also listed the bank as an organization that supported the NRA. Due to the significant political pressure, the bank decided to end the relationship.

It's not just individual candidates that can create political risk. There is also the risk of supporting or doing business with an organization that's controversial or becomes increasingly controversial.

"Customer feedback has caused us to review our relationship with the NRA," the bank announced via Twitter eight days after the shooting. "As a result, First National Bank of Omaha will not renew its contract with the National Rifle Association to issue the NRA Visa card."

It's unclear how this has impacted the bank. On the one hand, it appeased a large group of customers. On the other hand, the NRA's members are equally passionate and might be willing to end their relationship with the bank for failing to support their organization. While First National Bank couldn't have necessarily predicted this outcome, it should have considered the risk of having such a public relationship with an organization dealing with a hot button political issue. It's easy for everyone to get behind groups like the American Heart Association, St. Jude's Children's Hospital, or No Kid Hungry, but political causes can turn controversial quickly, inflaming feelings and alienating customers.

News reports don't say when First National Bank's relationship with the NRA began, but it likely happened in a different political climate. Perhaps because Nebraska was a "red state" the bank believed its customer base wouldn't blink at the arrangement. Whatever the reason, this kind of relationship posed a risk, and First National should have been assessing this risk every time its NRA contract came up for renewal, weighing the interchange income and revenue from the card program and customer lead generation with public opinion. Political climates change, which in turn shifts the level of associated political risk.

CONSTANT VIGILANCE

An institution's job isn't done once it identifies a risk facing an area or a business line. It must be regularly reviewing the risks the institutions face for changes and additions.

Consider the case of a Utah community bank that was surprised to discover that one of the offshore companies it provided aircraft registering services to in 2013 belonged to Russia's wealthiest oligarch and friend of Russian President Vladimir Putin, Leonid Mikhelson.

For years, the $1.1 billion-asset bank had made millions in fee income from its legal niche business line of helping foreigners legally register their aircraft in the United States. The leak of the so-called Paradise Papers (a trove of 13.4 million confidential documents from offshore law firm Appleby detailing offshore investments) to a German newspaper revealed the details of the company's ownership.

The bank began providing services to the company in 2013 and the next year the Treasury Department's Office of Foreign Assets Control sanctioned Mikhelson's energy company (but not Mikhelson himself) after

Russian military interference in Ukraine. While the bank says it knew the company's owner "was Russian," it didn't know much else since it was registered under Panamanian company Golden Star Aviation, *The New York Times* reports. When registration renewal time came, the bank permitted the renewal.

How did this happen?

Bank executives told the Times "that Mr. Mikhelson's case escaped scrutiny during an earlier period when their internal review process was less rigorous," and they vowed to review it.

"Russian involvement would score as a high risk by itself," a bank executive told the paper. "It's highly unlikely that something like this would have been approved in today's climate."

This raises an important point about risk management and how we need to make sure past decisions match up with today's standards, especially if those decisions are still the last word on existing products, services, and relationships. Risk management has evolved dramatically over the past decade, and the world that influences our decisions has changed even faster. We are constantly learning about new threats, challenges, and opportunities. A successful institution needs systems in place to ensure that identifying and addressing these developments is baked into the way it does business, not an afterthought to be brought up when a problem is found.

CHAPTER FIVE

WHY GOVERNANCE MATTERS

Risk creates accountability.

I n 2008 researchers in Japan devised an experiment to test how ano-nymity impacts rule breaking.[50] They divided participants into four groups to play a coin flipping game in private. Two groups were told to anonymously report their results while the other two were instructed to write their name and student ID on their reporting sheet. Half of the participants were told they'd be rewarded with a coupon book worth about $5 if they won. The others were not incentivized.

The laws of probability dictate that there's a 25 percent chance that participants would get heads or tails two times in a row and win the game. Yet 46 percent of anonymous students claimed they'd won the prize compared to just 21 percent of identified participants. Even the anonymous participants with no prize at stake reported winning at a statistically unlikely rate: 35 percent claimed to have won.

In a surprise to no one who has ever read the comments section of a website, the study results make it clear that anonymity gives many people a green light to engage in antisocial behavior. Why do they do this? There is no accountability for their actions. There is no oversight. There is no risk of being caught.

Risk creates accountability. It makes people and institutions more cautious because they are held responsible for the results.

71

FAILING TO ACCOUNT FOR RISK

There's no need to create an experiment to test this concept in the banking world. The industry has done a good job demonstrating the point on its own, particularly in the mortgage crisis that helped cause The Great Recession.

Remember Washington Mutual?

In the mid-2000s it was the sixth-largest bank in the country, ultimately reaching $307 billion in assets when it finally failed under the weight of subprime mortgages losses.

WaMu's downfall was its high-risk lending strategy. As home prices and demand for mortgage-backed securities rose, the bank saw an opportunity in the subprime and alternative mortgage marketplace. Borrowers couldn't afford the homes they wanted with traditional 30-year fixed-rate mortgages. Higher risk loans, like option adjustable-rate mortgages and cash-out refinances that let customers take out negatively amortizing mortgages, filled a market need for consumers who didn't always understand how their loans worked.

Meanwhile, because these loans had higher rates, they were worth more than 30-year mortgages when the bank sold them to investors. If a borrower didn't pay the full amount of the loan, the bank could count the accrued interest as profits. Better yet, from WaMu's short-sighted perspective, because someone else bought the loans, the risky loans were off the bank's books. If a loan defaulted, it would be someone else's problem.

With risk seemingly off the table, WaMu dove into high-risk lending, pursuing profits. Brokers were rewarded for closing ARMs with much higher commissions than traditional mortgages, motivating many to push the loans on customers, including those who might have been eligible for a fixed-rate loan. The more productive the loan officer, the greater the rewards, including trips to Hawaii as part of the bank's President's Club for top performers.

Executives also raked in the cash. The loans increased the bank's profits, which in turn boosted executive bonuses. Former chairman and CEO Kerry Killinger earned $19 million in 2005 and $24 million in 2006. Shareholders were rewarded with climbing stock prices.

Since WaMu didn't retain the risk for the loans, it wasn't concerned about underwriting. Documentation of income was minimal and often nonexistent. In one case reported by *The New York Times,* a loan officer counted a photo of a borrower in a mariachi costume as documentation of the six-figure income the singer claimed. The bank actively encouraged appraisers to inflate the value of homes so that loans looked more solid and valuable to investors and purchased questionable subprime loans from other originators. It even packaged loans it knew were destined for default and sold them without telling investors about its internal analysis.

Management knew about this fraud and didn't care. It repeatedly ignored reports about fraudulent documents and misrepresentations in mortgages it originated. Those inside the company tasked with managing risk were blatantly ignored.

"WaMu knowingly implemented a High Risk Lending Strategy, but failed to establish a corresponding system for risk management," concludes a U.S. Senate report on the financial collapse. "Instead, it marginalized risk managers who warned about and attempted to limit the risk associated with the high risk strategy."[51]

But ignoring risk is not an effective strategy. When the secondary market for mortgage-backed securities dried up in August 2007, WaMu had nowhere to sell its toxic mortgages and began to take on millions in losses. In the first quarter of 2008, WaMu lost $1.14 billion and half of its stock's value. That September, facing $180 billion in mortgage losses, regulators seized the bank and sold it to JPMorgan.

It was an ugly ending to a risky strategy, but it wasn't a unique one. Wachovia faced a similar end, being snapped up by Wells Fargo. Investment banks like Merrill Lynch and Bear Stearns were caught up in the carnage of risky decision making. It all came down to ignoring risk.

Ignoring or not fully understanding risk was a rampant problem which ultimately culminated in the financial crisis. Surprisingly, this was particularly true at big banks that employed chief risk officers (CROs). Researchers looked at use of the riskiest derivatives at 157 of the largest U.S. banks between 1995 and 2010. They found that those with CROs were far more likely to have been overexposed.[52] This was attributed to several causes. First, risk managers were not tasked with policing risk.

Their job was to fully maximize risk-adjusted returns, encouraging them to use risky instruments to bring the bank to the estimated limit of its risk-return strategy. They also suggested that a CRO gave everyone else at the bank "moral license" not to worry about risk, having mentally outsourced the task to the CRO. Finally, CEOs who were compensated by cash bonuses rather than stock were more interested in short-term gains and were eager to exploit derivatives.

As the study authors wrote in an article for *Harvard Business Review,* "When they had more skin in the game — for example, if they held a lot of stock in the company — they restrained the CRO's push for risky derivatives. But the opposite was true when CEOs received more compensation in the form of performance pay (like a big cash bonus), which rewards outsize risk taking but doesn't penalize losses."[53]

The behavior of these CEOs demonstrates yet again the connection between risk and accountability. When a stakeholder thinks he has little to lose and plenty to gain for his actions, he will often make a bad decision. But as we're beginning to see, just because someone thinks there's no risk to engaging in a certain course of action doesn't mean there aren't consequences. When you ignore risk, you're not just ignoring the obvious risks that are right in front of you. You're also ignoring the broad range of potential side effects that can come back to haunt you.

WaMu's cautionary tale is a classic example of what happens when financial institutions don't evaluate risk when calculating strategic decisions. Banks are evaluated by return on equity and their ability to generate income for shareholders. When the opportunity arose to increase fee income with exotic mortgage products, including ARMs and home equity refinancing with higher interest rates, suddenly the 30-year fixed-rate mortgages that had been the industry standard for decades were no longer appealing. Conforming mortgages were less risky, but they also had a smaller return. With banks able to offload risk onto investors by securitizing mortgages, they didn't care if mortgages were high-risk, as long as they generated higher profits.

The reason why 30-year fixed-rate mortgages have been and are once again the gold standard of mortgage lending is because of the risk profile. Carefully underwritten with ample documentation and down payments, it's the type of loan that institutions are comfortable leaving on their books. When risk belongs to an institution, it chooses to make loans that fit within its risk tolerance and overall strategic plan.

When fees are the only thing an institution is looking at, exotic mortgage products are appealing. But when an institution is incorporating risk into its decision making, conforming 30-year fixed-rate mortgages suddenly look like a much safer and more intelligent investment. They may not boost profits with large amounts of fee income today, but they can be reliable source of income that, when combined with the right risk strategy, function as a long-term profitable business line.

When you ignore risk, you're not just ignoring the obvious risks that are right in front of you. You're also ignoring the broad range of potential side effects that can come back to haunt you.

PREVENTING SCANDALS WITH GOVERNANCE & OVERSIGHT

A common theme throughout the Senate report on WaMu's failure was a board and management that systematically ignored and isolated risk managers. Those that tried to sound alarm bells were stripped of their authority and left out of key meetings. While a risk management program had been drafted, it was never executed because higher ups felt it got in the way of writing loans and making profits.

This slapdash approach to governance and oversight is a recipe for scandal. When a board and management adopt a strategic plan, they not only need to consider the potential risks of an action, but also need a plan to monitor and oversee the activity to ensure risks are being actively mitigated.

Unfortunately, there are times when management turns a blind eye to these duties, and the results can be disastrous. Just ask Wells Fargo. In 2016 the banking giant agreed to pay $185 million in fines and fire 5,300 employees after thousands of employees secretly opened over 2 million deposit and credit card accounts for unwitting customers—transferring customers' funds into them and often collecting fees.[54]

It wasn't just a few bad apples. It was a systemic problem, which is one spurred by compensation incentives and intense pressure to meet sales goals. It sounds like a strategic plan gone wrong due to lack of risk management.

Ignoring risk (and risk managers) is not an effective strategy.

It likely began with a strategic plan to increase checking and credit card account openings. Someone decided that incentivizing the workforce would boost account openings. Management agreed the idea sounded good and proceeded with it without considering the potential risk. Had Wells Fargo taken the time to engage in risk management, it might have realized the potential for employees to abuse the system and built safeguards to prevent it. It could have drafted strong account opening and management policies and procedures and put a system in place to ensure those policies and procedures were followed.

Clearly, it didn't. In a Barclays Global Financial Services Conference Call, Wells Fargo CFO John Shrewsberry commented that employee terminations "were results of our own internal investigations as part of our internal controls and did not happen all at once but took place over the last five years. The terminations have declined every year since 2013 but on an annual basis represented approximately 1% of the team members that worked in our stores each year.[55]

The key phrase here is "over the last five years." Wells Fargo knew it had a widespread, systemic problem violating customer trust for five years, and it let the problem continue. Sure, it had ethics workshops telling employees not to invent fictional bank accounts for customers and it hired "risk professionals," but if it knew employees were skirting protocols, certainly it could have adopted a stronger, more accountable system for monitoring new accounts. It shouldn't be easy to hide fraud.

It seems like Wells Fargo wants to blame bad apple employees instead of its own failure to stop them. After all, it was the behemoth's own sales practices that spurred employees to abuse customers. Now Wells Fargo is paying the price in fines, lawsuits, bad publicity, and lost customer accounts.

WaMu and Wells Fargo are extreme examples of what can go wrong when a financial institution fails to properly align strategic planning with risk management. There are many ways to measure their failures, but it really all comes down to the company's value. Wells Fargo's stock was worth about $50 the day before news came out of the account-opening scandal. Soon after, the stock lost 12 percent of its value, reaching a two-year low and taking two months for the stock price to recover. WaMu was sold to JPMorgan Chase at the fire sale price of $1.9 billion and the holding company filed for bankruptcy.

That's a far cry from the 25 percent bump in valuation a company with strong enterprise risk management can expect.[56]

AVOIDING FRAUD WITH STRONG RISK MANAGEMENT GOVERNANCE

These scandals could have been prevented if the people in charge of overseeing the institutions were thinking independently and responsibly about the potential consequences. It comes down to strong governance, something these institutions lacked.

We've already talked about the role the board plays in setting an institution's risk tolerance, but that assumes that the board is well equipped to fill this role effectively and ethically. It assumes that the board takes it fiduciary responsibilities seriously. It assumes that when the management team is tasked with executing strategy, that they watch carefully to ensure that enterprise risk management is central to the process.

COSO reminds us that we must ensure the board has the skills, experience, and business knowledge to not take everything management says at face value. It isn't there to rubber stamp management's plans, but to serve as a sounding board and collaborator that asks tough questions and poses alternative strategies and scenarios to understand why the decisions being made are the best choice. If Enron's board had questioned management's excessive compensation or refused to let the company engage in billions of dollars of off-the-books activities, its story might have ended differently.

A good board has the knowledge, experience, and skills to understand and question management's decisions. Its knowledge and skills should evolve with the times and the challenges facing the institution. Should an institution shift strategies and move into more mortgage or real estate lending, board training must reflect that. The members need to understand how ERM works and how the institution's objectives match up with its risk taking and tolerance.

A good board has the knowledge, experience, and skills to understand and question management's decisions.

Just as important, a board needs to be independent and have no conflicts of interest. Board members need to be able to objectively evaluate the institution and its performance. While this can be difficult since board members at many small financial institutions include investors or customers, it's not impossible. Code of ethics policies should be drafted, reviewed, and strictly adhered to. Institutions must comply with Regulation O, which limits loans to insiders like board members and management and requires that such loans be disclosed in quarterly reports. Management and directors must also guard against one person holding too much power, a situation that invites fraud and abuse.

Just consider the case of bank director at a small community bank in Wisconsin who got called out in a consent order by the OCC for allegedly failing to properly oversee the CEO's compensation.

Sylvia Thoe, senior vice president and cashier at First National Bank in Waupaca, Wis., joined the bank's board, serving on the compensation committee. During her three years on the committee, Thoe did nothing to stop Archie Overby, the bank's former president, CEO, and chairman, from using bank funds for his personal expenses even though she was aware he'd done it before.[57] Overby spent over $1.6 million of the bank's funds to pay for luxury travel and other expenses[58] while the bank contracted 27 percent over five years (from $747 million to $548 million).

The OCC said Thoe also approved excessive compensation, with Overby's base salary "85 percent above the market 75th percentile base salary ($377,886)." This may have had something to do with the fact that Overby had borrowed more than $2 million from Thoe and her husband, a fact that she didn't disclose to other board members and that should have caused her to recuse herself from votes on his compensation.

While it's surprising to see a single director called out, it appears these were unusual circumstances with a particularly overbearing CEO. An outside consulting report noted "that Respondent [Overby] was 'the dominant influence in all aspects of Bank operations,' Respondent's decisions were 'rarely challenged credibly by other executive members of the Bank,' and Respondent's 'prior resistance to acknowledging and separation of duties and traditional controls has exposed the Bank to elevated risk.'"

Overby voted as a member of the compensation committee to give himself a raise, hired his son-in-law as controller and his successor before getting board approval, and paid his daughter $60,000 a year to work remotely even though she had another full-time job, among other abuses listed in the enforcement actions. Board members didn't know Overby was using bank funds to pay for luxury trips and other personal expenses and voted to approve an annual miscellaneous expense letter, assuming that it was all related to bank business.

This governance lesson for directors is a simple one: take the requirement to be independent seriously. Disclose conflicts of interest. If miscellaneous expenses seem exorbitant or something just doesn't make financial sense, ask questions and follow up. A good working relationship with management is essential, but that doesn't mean greenlighting every decision without thought.

Board members play a critical role in risk management but can only be effective when they are informed and inquisitive.

Board members play a critical role in risk management but can only be effective when they are informed and inquisitive.

OPERATING STRUCTURES

There is no single ideal operating structure suitable for every institution. Each institution has its own unique characteristics, including size, business lines, geography, complexity, etc., that influence how different entities are structured. COSO shows us that operating structures are one of the most important elements in ensuring that "authority, accountability, and responsibility" at all levels are plainly outlined and enforced and that communication lines are clear and open.

A centralized approach is far more effective in uncovering risks and finding how they connect than a decentralized approach that tends to focus more on putting out fires than seeing the big picture.

When it comes to ERM, COSO notes that a centralized approach is far more effective in uncovering risks and finding how they connect than a decentralized approach that tends to focus more on putting out fires than seeing the big picture. The structure also needs to keep pace with a risk management environment that is constantly evolving. That includes:

Independent reviews. It's not enough to have a risk management process. That process needs to be effective and remain consistent with the FI's overall business strategy. An independent review objectively assesses an institution's risk management controls to determine if they are effectively mitigating risk. Management must tell the board when significant weaknesses are found so it can decide whether to deploy new resources or consider a new approach.

Documentation. If it's not written down, it didn't happen. The institution should keep all enterprise risk management documentation organized. This includes everything produced by the board, management, and employees. Documents should be up to date and readily available to facilitate the oversight, accountability, and monitoring of risk management.

Oversight and accountability. Effective oversight requires that roles and responsibilities are clearly defined, that individuals given tasks have the knowledge, authority, and resources to complete them, and that there is a system in place to integrate ERM into the institution's everyday activities. The board, senior management, and staff each have a role to play, and there needs to be a way to track what each party is responsible for and what they have done to address it:

> **Board.** The board is responsible for the bank's overall ERM process, including all five elements of the COSO ERM model. It's tasked with ensuring that the institution's mission, vision, and core values align with strategy and the creation of risk management structure, which may include audit, risk, compensation, or governance committees. As the chief promoter of the institution's risk management culture, it needs to develop ways to promote a risk-aware mindset throughout the institution. It sets the institution's risk tolerance and approves risk policies and plans. It reviews due diligence results and ongoing monitoring to be aware of the most significant issues affecting the institution and ensure they are remediated. They're also responsible for proactively asking questions and challenging assumptions.

> **Management.** COSO's "lines of accountability model" gives ultimate responsibility for strategy and business objectives to the chief executive officer (CEO). While the board is responsible for setting strategy and risk tolerances, the CEO is in charge of execution, developing plans and processes for managing risk, and presenting them to the board. The CEO conducts due diligence and reports findings to the board.

The CEO leads a management team, creating an environment of risk awareness that should trickle down to frontline employees. The makeup of management varies by the size and complexity of an institution. While a large institution may have a broad management team with everything from a chief risk officer, chief compliance officer, chief audit officer, and chief information officer, these roles may be combined at smaller institutions. In some cases, the CEO may even be the chief risk officer. Some will have large risk committees while a smaller management team may require that everyone attend risk meetings.

Committees & departments. Unlike management, the board isn't living risk management on a day-to-day basis. Committees are the go-between that allow the board members in committees to ask additional questions and understand what's going on. Committees increase the likelihood that the overall board will truly understand a topic like risk management.

Committees composed of board members and focused on a specific topic create an environment where board members can do a deep dive to get the information they need to understand trends and inform decisions around areas such as strategy or resource needs. When board members serve on committees, they develop specialized knowledge that makes the board stronger as a whole. No single board member can be an expert on everything. While every board member should be familiar with risk management, committees ensure that at least a few members have the kind of insightful knowledge that goes beyond the basic principles. These committees can provide an overall status report on risk management to the board while keeping an eye on emerging trends that may not yet require the full board's attention.

Departments, lines of business, or functional areas are responsible for executing the tasks assigned by management. They do the work of developing and monitoring controls to mitigate risk. They work together using a common language to understand risk and vendor management across various departments. They need to report their progress up the ladder.

Departments should have their own meetings separate from committees where they talk about what they've done, what needs to be done, and provide information to department heads who will relay the most important material to the board or its committees.

A liaison from management should compile and manage committee meetings. This might be the risk officer or compliance officer or a combination of the two. The person selected must be able to provide information from across different departments.

The committee needs to be able to take all the information and determine what it means. How does it all come together? What matters to the institution? The liaison should be able to take all the line of business or functional-area information and organize it in a way that prioritizes the most significant reports and data.

While committees need information from many departments to get a full picture of risk and vendor management, not every department head needs to be on the committee. It depends on the institution's culture and structure.

Some institutions want everyone to feel important and involved. They want to limit surprises, so they invite every department head to be part of the risk committee. That's not realistic. Instead, departments should have their own meetings and report on what they've done, and boards should be limited to a few key individuals.

When properly structured, departments provide the on-the-ground information that inform the board's decision making.

Under no circumstances should a chief risk officer be the only person at an institution tasked with managing risk. It's an enterprise-wide endeavor, one that benefits from the management and expertise of a talented chief risk officer but that requires a team effort to be effective.

Committees increase the likelihood that the overall board will truly understand a topic like risk management.

Employees. An institution's employees are responsible for monitoring risk and informing management if monitoring reveals problems, whether it's an increase in risk, system failure, or compliance issues. Not only should they be properly trained, but their knowledge should be leveraged to improve risk management practices. Employees should be accountable for following all risk management policies and procedures.

Frontline employees can serve as important risk management controls. Just ask HSBC. A teller in one of the bank's London branches was able to do what Angola's government couldn't: recognize a $500 million scam. An accountant came into the branch asking to transfer $2 million to an account in Japan. The teller was surprised to see a $500 million account balance, and asked a few questions of the customer. Unsatisfied with the answers, she declined the transfer and alerted her bosses, according to an investigation in *The Wall Street Journal*.[59] It turns out the money came from Angola's central bank reserves and was headed to scammers who'd used fraudulent documents to rip off the government.

How to Set Up a Risk Committee

Risk management is all about knowledge. When you know the threats and opportunities across the enterprise, you can leverage that information to make the best decisions. The board determines the FI's risk appetite, develops a strategic plan that takes risk into account, and approves how risk is governed. The heavy lifting of identifying, assessing, measuring, monitoring, and mitigating risk falls to management.

The risk committee is the go-between that helps ensure management and the board understand each other. It lets board members ask questions and ensures management gets clear marching orders.

Crafting a charter

The charter (or bylaws) outlines the responsibilities and expectations of the risk committee. Charters should be detailed to increase consistency and the committee's value. There is no one right way to write a charter, but it should include:

Expectations. The committee oversees risk management, but what does that mean? Define the committee's parameters and powers. This can be very specific or a broad mandate to cover risk at a high-level. Specify what kind of decision-making authority the committee has. That might include authority to make strategic decisions about how to track and communicate risk and what kind of resources will be allocated. What types of materials should it review, and how are deliberation results tracked and shared? The committee should define the responsibilities of management, whether that's minimum standards or fully fleshed out duties.

Committee members. The makeup of the committee depends on the culture and environment. The risk committee commonly has two board members, but that's not a hard and fast rule. A financial institution can put as many board members on the committee as it wants, depending on its environment and culture.

There also needs to be representation from the C-suite. Sometimes it's the risk officer and CEO for dual control. Other times, when a risk officer has been with the CEO for a long time and has a strong relationship, it might be okay to have the CRO meet without the CEO. Other times the CEO needs to serve as a buffer or guide the message because they are not on the same page as the risk officer. Consider the political factors at your institution.

You don't want every member of the C-suite on the committee. Too many individuals will only increase debate and hurt productivity. The goal is to avoid surprises by having the most appropriate voices represented.

Meeting frequency and notification. Determine how often the committee should meet, who can call a meeting, and how much notice will be required. The risk committee should meet at least quarterly. It's also a good idea to empower board committee members to call an ad hoc or immediate committee session. Determine how much notice is required, whether it's 8 hours, 12 hours, or some other time period. Decide how far in advance agendas must be provided.

Quorum. How many committee members need to be at a meeting for it to be official? How many board members need to be present? Minutes must be taken.

Location. Must meetings be held in person, or can they be conducted virtually or over the phone? The charter might require at least one in-person meeting over a calendar year.

When drafting a charter, it's fine to look at other institutions' charters, but it's important to customize it to your own institution. Every institution has a different approach to risk management depending on its size, risk appetite, business lines, and other factors. Adopting another institution's charter may mean including elements that aren't applicable to you. Whatever you borrow must be germane to your resources, abilities, and what you do.

Ultimately, the board should approve all charters, including the charter for the risk committee.

AUDIT COMMITTEES

An audit committee provides oversight of the audit process and the internal controls it reviews. Are audit committees a regulatory requirement or just a best practice? It depends on the size and type of your financial institution.

Banks and credit unions have different regulatory requirements and expectations for their audit and supervisory committees. Institution size can also impact expectations for how audit committees are composed.

Regulatory Expectation: Does Your FI Need an Audit Committee?

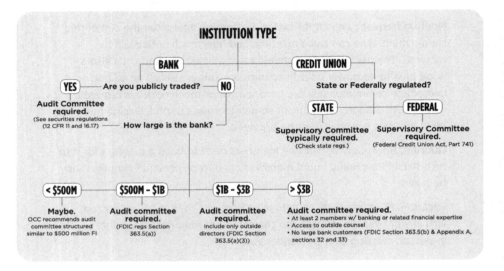

BANKS

Audit committees are a good practice and sometimes even required by regulation.

Banks with $500 million or more in assets. Section 363.5(a) of the FDIC's regulations requires federally insured banks with $500 million or more in assets to have a dedicated audit committee.

Banks with less than $500 million in assets. For those under the asset threshold, the OCC encourages banks to have a similarly structured audit committee.

Banks with $1 billion or more in assets. Institutions with $1 billion or more in assets have additional composition requirements. Generally, only outside directors (independent of management) should be part of the audit committee. Section 363.5(a)(3) defines an outside director as an individual who is not, and within the preceding year has not been, an officer or employee of the institution or any affiliate of the institution.

In addition, the FDIC's Guidelines to Part 363 provide that the board of directors should determine annually whether all existing and potential audit committee members are independent of management. The guidelines also describe the factors that should be considered when making this determination.

Banks with $3 billion or more in assets. The FDIC rule requires that these banks' audit committees include:

1. At least 2 members with banking or related financial management expertise
2. Access to outside counsel
3. No large customers of the bank

These criteria are all described in section 363.5(b) and in Appendix A, sections 32 and 33.

Publicly traded banks. Public reporting banks should also understand securities regulations (12 CFR 11 and 16.17) that impose specific audit committee requirements.

CREDIT UNIONS

Federal credit unions are required to have a supervisory committee per the Federal Credit Union Act. Most federally insured state-chartered credit unions have similar requirements dictated by state statute or regulation. State-chartered credit unions may find slight differences in their own statutes and regulations, but all federally insured credit unions must follow the audit and verification requirements for Supervisory Committees found in Part 741.

A credit union's supervisory committee is essentially its audit committee. This is reflected in the requirements that the supervisory committee performs an annual audit and submit an audit report to the board of directors and the members during the annual meeting of the credit union.

The composition of the Supervisory Committee is a statutory matter. The Federal Credit Union Act requires that the board of directors appoints a committee with three to five members, one of whom may be an uncompensated director. Additional limitations on who may serve on the supervisory committee may be found in your credit union bylaws (e.g., employees and certain officers may not serve).

The now-retired NCUA Supervisory Committee Guide provides excellent insights into the type of background and skills members of the Supervisory Committee should possess:

1.   Be a member of the credit union
2.   Be bondable by the credit union's surety bond company
3.   Experience in bookkeeping, accounting, or auditing is recommended

The bottom line on audit committees: Audit committees are generally required by regulation and are also a best practice. They are an integral component of the safety and soundness of a financial institution. Audit committee members should be supported through continuous training in accounting and risk management.

Regardless of whether an institution has an audit committee, it needs to have an audit function involved in risk management.

Firms are accomplishing risk governance in many ways, according to a report by EY.[60] "Firms are adding new board-level committees to more closely monitor business ethics and conduct, and many are restructuring internally—streamlining and integrating current management committees, adding new committees and functions—to break down silos and close the gaps in risk oversight and control. Many are strengthening their three lines of defense to clarify roles and responsibilities, redesigning frameworks to shift risk accountability to the front line."

Every institution needs to examine its own risks, opportunities, and resources to determine the best methodology for strong enterprise risk management.

CHAPTER SIX

BUILDING A RISK MANAGEMENT CULTURE

A risk management culture doesn't just prevent fraud. It also encourages the institution to consider the consequences of its actions from a risk management perspective.

In 2013, British banking firm Barclays had a real problem on its hands. Barclays was one of several banks tasked with helping calculate the London Interbank Offered Rate (LIBOR) and the Euribor by submitting its borrowing costs.

But that's not what Barclays did.

Between 2005 and 2009, the bank frequently let traders influence its reported LIBOR rate, at the time a critically important benchmark interest rate, manipulating it to benefit Barclays' own derivative positions. For instance, the U.S. Commodity Futures Trading Commission (CFTC), which ending up fining Barclays $200 million for its wrongdoing, shared the example of one trader who emailed, "We have another big fixing tomorrow and with the market move I was hoping we could set [certain] LIBORs as high as possible." Those in charge of submitting LIBOR and other rates would typically agree with emailed responses such as "always happy to help," "for you, anything," or "Done...for you big boy."[61]

This happened "on numerous occasions and sometimes on a daily basis over a four-year period," the CFTC found. The problem was traced all the way to senior management. When the press began wondering why Barclays' borrowing costs were so much higher than its peers, management requested those in charge of submitting LIBOR rates to make the rates lower to draw less attention to the bank's activity, particularly as the financial crisis was bringing down other banks. There was even a phrase for it: heads above the parapet.

It's a pretty stupid thing to do, isn't it? Barclays was worried that people wouldn't trust the stability and credibility of the firm while investment banks around the world floundered because its lies were too big. To protect its credibility and maintain the public's trust, Barclay's *adjusted its lies to make them less noticeable.* What could go wrong?

I'll give you one guess.

Barclays was found out, suffering massive damage to its reputation. Regulators pounced. The public howled. The CEO lost his job. The damage was so bad that Barclays' board took an unusual step. It commissioned a firm to study what went wrong with the bank to allow such insidious actions and how to fix it. Then it published the results for the world to read.

The resulting 244-page Salz Review[62] by lawyer and former British Broadcasting Corporation (BBC) vice chairman Anthony Salz took the bank to task for many things, but at the top of the list was its culture. Barclays' lacked a purpose other than growth and financial success, leading to a poor outcome where the focus on customers was forgotten. Instead "They should promote standards that support Barclays' ambition to be seen as a leader in business practices among its peer institutions and multi-national corporates generally. The senior leadership team should be responsible for demonstrating and promoting these high standards. This should be reflected in their annual evaluations and variable compensation."

Employees weren't encouraged to speak up when something was wrong. In fact, one employee who objected to misreporting figures but had no other choice, wrote to his supervisor, "following on from my conversation with you I will reluctantly, gradually and artificially get my LIBORs in line with the rest of the contributors as requested. I disagree with this approach as you are well aware. I will be contributing rates which are nowhere near the clearing rates for unsecured cash and therefore will not be posting honest prices."[63]

Barclays only sporadically promoted any type of values and never across the whole organization, which was made more challenging thanks to its rapid growth. It also didn't include values in employee evaluations except for the concept of "winning." It also had a poor record for dealing with customer complaints. The board received little information about the bank's culture.

By now we've all figured out what happens when there isn't a culture of risk management at a financial institution: there is some *other* kind of culture, and often it's one with a negative influence.

Remember Wells Fargo and how its sales culture caused the account opening scandal? It's just one example in a sea of dysfunctional corporate cultures. Let's go back to the big fraud that helped inspire the need for COSO's ERM framework in the first place: Enron.

As C. William Thomas relates in *Journal of Accountancy*,[64] as Enron found more and more success in energy derivatives and other questionable contracts, it's "internal culture apparently began to take a darker tone."

> "[Enron CEO Jeff] Skilling instituted the performance review committee (PRC), which became known as the harshest employee-ranking system in the country. It was known as the '360-degree review' based on the values of Enron—respect, integrity, communication and excellence (RICE). However, associates came to feel that the only real performance measure was the amount of profits they could produce. In order to achieve top ratings, everyone in the organization became instantly motivated to 'do deals' and post earnings. Employees were regularly rated on a scale of 1 to 5, with 5s usually being fired within six months. The lower an employee's PRC score, the closer he or she got to Skilling, and the higher the score, the closer he or she got to being shown the door. Skilling's division was known for replacing up to 15% of its workforce every year. Fierce internal competition prevailed and immediate gratification was prized above long-term potential. Paranoia flourished and trading contracts began to contain highly restrictive confidentiality clauses. Secrecy became the order of the day for many of the company's trading contracts, as well as its disclosures."[65]

This behavior isn't limited to a few bad apples.

One survey of 500 financial services professionals in the United States and the United Kingdom found that a quarter believed that to be successful they'd have to engage in "unethical or illegal conduct" and a third felt pressured to do so by bonus or compensation plans.[66] Meanwhile a Deloitte study of senior bankers found that 65 percent believe there are significant cultural problems in the industry and 33 percent reported a problem at their own bank.[67] This was especially true at investment banks compared to retail banks. Respondents believed the top five cultural problems were compensation structure; board oversight; compensation levels; lax capital rules; and management's risk understanding.

A risk management culture doesn't just prevent fraud. It also encourages the institution to consider the consequences of its actions from a risk management perspective. In 2017 the Consumer Financial Protection Bureau[68] sued $21.1 billion-asset TCF National Bank, based in Wayzata, Minn., for "tricking consumers into costly overdraft services in order to preserve its bottom line." The bank denied the allegations, saying it did not violate the unfair, deceptive, or abusive acts or practices (UDAAP) provisions of the Consumer Financial Protection Act. The CFPB settled the case for $25 million in restitution and a $5 million civil money penalty.[69]

The suit, which includes the testimony of former employees, says that the bank was so determined to protect its $180 million overdraft revenue stream after the Federal Reserve's "Opt-in Rule" took effect in 2010 that it took a page from the Wells Fargo handbook and incentivized employees to convince customers to opt in. Rewards included bonuses of up to $7,000 for some branch managers. After the bank discontinued the incentives program in 2011, some branch employees were required to meet an opt-in goal of 80 percent of all new accounts, the suit alleges. Many believed they would lose their jobs if they fell short, the CFPB said, including one former employee who said she was put on probation because only half her customers opted in.

But that's not all. The bank also systematically tested consumer responses to craft a script designed to imply that overdraft opt-in was mandatory for customers opening new accounts, the lawsuit alleges. The CFPB says TCF Bank went after existing customers too, asking them if they wanted their "TCF Check Card to continue to work as it does today" and assuming that saying yes meant they were opting into the overdraft program.

The bank also used "emotionally charged hypotheticals" suggesting that failure to have the service could leave them stranded on the side of the road or unable to buy food, the CFPB says.

These methods were effective, the CFPB says, helping TCF convince about 66 percent of customers to opt into the overdraft program at a rate that was more than triple than the average bank. It also collected hundreds of thousands of dollars in overdraft fees.

While the bank wanted to preserve revenue, it failed to consider the risk of its aggressive approach, both from a compliance and reputational risk perspective.

How, then, do we create a risk management culture? It begins by understanding the building blocks of culture.

WHAT IS CULTURE?

A culture of risk management is a top-down exercise in developing policies, procedures, messaging, and compensation that supports the institution's long-term goals, while front-line employees take an active role in managing risk.

Some institutions are risk averse while others take a more aggressive stance. Neither is necessarily right nor wrong, as long as the institution has carefully considered the potential impact of its decision. For instance, a mortgage bank is likely to have a more conservative approach to risk than an investment bank that trades derivatives. Similarly, what one institution views as a risk, another might view as an opportunity. What's important is that the institution has carefully aligned its goals, mission, and vision with its risk tolerance for long-term success.

But as the above examples have shown, this isn't always the case.

The Federal Reserve Bank of New York has spent years studying how to improve the culture at financial institutions and holds an annual culture conference. It has distilled corporate culture into three key issues:[70]

1. **Defining and clarifying purpose to create clear goals for assessing performance.** An institution's purpose should "emphasize sustainable success, not short-run profit." Customers should be at the center of business decisions. Stewardship should be a value of the institution.

The Fed isn't the only one to draw this conclusion. As a research review in Appendix B of the Salz Report points out, "Groups of people require (in a sociopsychological sense) that sense of purpose (what they are there to do). In this way, purpose is a foundation of culture. Culture then gets determined by the way the group shares and acts upon its collective sense of purpose. The research also shows that cultures defined by overly commercial and competitive features, with little regard for other elements, lead to poor outcomes."

This purpose needs to be clearly communicated by the board, which needs to follow up with management to ensure they are leading in a way that supports the institution's purpose. There must be consequences for those that stray.

2. **Measuring how firms and the industry are performing.** An institution needs to know if it's achieving its purpose and how it compares to its peers. Standardized metrics can be useful tools that assess behavior and culture, while including behavior in performance reviews can help influence behavior.

   William C. Dudley, president and CEO of the Federal Reserve Bank of New York thinks the industry would benefit from a "common culture survey" to benchmark behavior. Taking inspiration from an annual review of the United Kingdom's Banking Standards Board, he'd like to see banks ask whether employees agree with statements like:

   - "I believe senior leaders in my organization mean what they say."
   - "In my organization we are encouraged to follow the spirit of the rules (what they mean, not just the words)."
   - "I see people in my organization turn a blind eye to inappropriate behavior."
   - "If I raised concerns about the way we work, I would be worried about the negative consequences for me.

3. **Determining whether incentives encourage behaviors consistent with goals.** Incentives need to align with behaviors that will support long-term business goals.

The benefit of this is twofold, according to an article in the *Delaware Journal of Corporate Law*. There is the obvious problem we've seen before where employees put their own careers and monetary gain ahead of customer and institutional needs. The other problem is that incentives and policies that encourage employees to look out for their own interests instead of the institution can attract "individuals with anti-social traits" who can negatively influence others, creating a rash of bad behavior that spreads across an institution.

CULTURE & RISK MANAGEMENT

It's no surprise that one of the most substantial revisions to COSO's enterprise risk management framework is its new emphasis on culture. In its years of research and outreach, it must have come across findings from a multitude of studies and observers.

Some of the clearest observations of best practices come from the Salz Report which suggests, "The lessons from other high-risk industries include fostering a culture where: leadership and operational discipline is focused on areas of highest risk; speaking up and working collaboratively with regulators and with other stakeholders is encouraged; and risks and the appropriateness of business practices are continually evaluated."

These views are all reflected in the COSO framework. COSO suggests several qualities are needed in a risk-aware culture, one where accountability, behavior, and action all support the bank's core values. An institution needs to define its desired culture and demonstrate a commitment to core values. Remember, these are the fundamental beliefs and ideals of the institution that serve as a guidepost to help the institution determine what is right or wrong when making both big picture and everyday decisions. Judgement plays an important role. Leaders need the knowledge, experience, and insight into the institution's risk tolerance to make decisions efficiently, particularly in crisis situations. Risk tolerance should influence how an institution approaches everything from setting strategy and identifying risks to deploying resources and responding to changing conditions. It should be an intrinsic part of every strategic decision.

A risk management culture cannot simply be dictated. It must be embraced. It begins with strong leadership. Employees should feel a part of the risk management process. Managers should decide how risk should impact employees' roles and jobs. They should be encouraged to get involved in risk discussions and decision-making. Incentives should align with the institution's risk tolerance, and institutions should be responsive and non-punitive when someone points out a problem. In addition to policies, rules, and standards there should also be clear accountability and timely consequences for falling short.

Communication is critical from expectations to successes and failures. This is equally true at all levels of the institution including the front-line, midlevel, management, and board. Each party needs complete and accurate information to make risk-appropriate decisions.

The final cultural principle COSO addresses is human capital and the importance of attracting, developing, and retaining capable individuals. It's no secret that there is a shortage of top talent in the banking world, which can complicate the search for employees with a strong risk management background. Judgement skills and risk management experience should be an important factor when hiring for the C-level. For mid and lower-level positions, institutions can seek out candidates who aren't just competent, but have a background and personality traits that suggest they work collaboratively and are open-minded and inquisitive. Training should reinforce procedures, positive behaviors, and values while mentoring should focus on how their skills fit within the organization. Performance reviews should measure employee performance and provide incentives to retain them. Remember, incentives should align with the institution's long-term goals and objectives. Don't reward short-term behavior that runs counter to the long-term interests of the institution.

CREATING VALUE WITH RISK MANAGEMENT CULTURE

There is evidence that a risk management culture is taking hold at more institutions. A 2017 PwC survey found 55 percent of board members, C-level executives, and their direct reports have defined their risk appetite/tolerance across key categories. Fifty-one percent have a well-defined and well-communicated risk appetite. That's up from 42 percent and 38 percent in 2015, respectively.[71] Meanwhile nearly three quarters of chief risk officers say senior management "understand[s] the value of strong risk management," up from 58 percent in 2016.

No matter how bright and organized a chief risk officer is, an institution's ERM program is only effective when employees follow it. That's why building buy-in is essential for anyone involved in managing risk. In fact, it's the biggest challenge some CROs face.

In researching this book, I spoke with numerous risk officers, including one who manages strategic risk at a $1 billion+ community bank. More than anything, she struggles with getting everything she needs from busy business units that have clients to serve and profits to earn. It's been particularly tricky over the past few years as the bank has upgraded its ERM process and other elements of its risk management program. Yet she's been proactive and is making progress, she says.

The banker is quick to clarify that she isn't the bank's CRO. Her job is to help implement the bank's risk management strategies while playing a critical role in operations. The CRO job technically falls to the CEO, who is a huge advocate for risk management along with the bank's chief operating officer. Their support is essential to her success, she says.

"I have the authority to talk to committees and tremendous support from the top down in terms of risk," she says of the autonomy she's given. "There is absolutely no tolerance for not supporting any risk-related discussion."

While the banker typically has everyone's attention when a major change is rolled out, it doesn't last forever. Changes soon become old news and can get lost in the shuffle. Also, not everyone understands the tools available. Consider a senior credit officer on the operational risk management committee. He was discussing concentration risk when the banker asked him if he'd used the bank's system to create an easy-to-track finding.

His response: "No. I'm working on Key Risk Indicators, but I'm also working on *real* risk."

They should be one and the same, notes the risk manager, and that's the next level of risk management for the bank. Staff needs to understand the system isn't just busy work meant to make pretty reports. Fully utilizing the bank's ERM tools and solution will ultimately make the credit risk officer's job easier while improving the bank's long-term risk management.

To overcome this problem, the bank now requires every management committee to include dashboards from the bank's ERM systems as an agenda item in every meeting, forcing them to begin using the tool for reporting. It also prevents the risk manager from being the sole spokesperson for everything risk: the message comes from the top.

Risk management fatigue also sets into meetings. It's easy to look back at dashboards to see past findings, the banker says, but it's just as important to look ahead to emerging risks. She tackled this problem recently by reformatting meetings. She added look-back reporting to the consent agenda, which is sent in advance. This gives members time to send in questions and concerns, leaving more time for meaningful discussion.

While the bank and the risk manager have come a long way, building buy-in will remain a work in progress as the bank continues on its journey to improve its overall ERM.

"Every time I listen to speakers around enterprise risk or regulator boards and panels and hear them talk about different aspects of managing risk I come back and tell my bosses 'We've done so much, but we still have so much left to do,'" she says.

In the end, a strong risk management culture is all about leadership and that leadership creates value. The Deloitte report *The Leadership Premium* found that the long-term equity value of a company perceived as having good leadership could increase by as much as 37 percent for financial services companies.[72] An institution where leaders regularly demonstrate the core value of stewardship should fare much better than one where people know it is merely lip service.

CHAPTER SEVEN

RISK ANALYSIS & EVALUATION

Once risks are identified and assessed, an institution needs to be sure it understands those risks.

B y now it's obvious that risk plays a critical role in strategic deci- sion-making. However, acknowledging that risk exists is just the first step in the risk analysis and evaluation process. Circumstances are constantly changing, and the risk an institution faces changes along with the world around it. An institution should be regularly monitoring both the upside and downside of risk, shoring up potential weaknesses and seeking out new opportunities.

That's why it's essential to have metrics for measuring and managing risk. Risk monitoring and assessments are a critical part of an ERM program, enabling institutions to measure performance. Effective risk monitoring is a collaborative activity that helps an institution understand its efforts to address both known and emerging risks across the entire institution.

An institution's risk measuring and monitoring program should be built around its enterprise risk assessment and the key risks it has identified. Every institution faces a variety of risks, but not all risks have the same consequences. For example, it's bad if a customer slips on a patch of ice in the parking lot because the vendor used for plowing did a lousy job. There's the risk that the institution may be sued for the accident. It's an unwanted lawsuit, but in the scale of things, it would be much worse if hackers gained access to sensitive customer information. Similarly, some risks impact different business lines and areas of the bank with varying degrees of severity. A risk may impact one area of the institution, but not make it necessary to rethink the overall strategy. In other cases, risks can combine to create situations that require adjustments to strategic goals and objectives. A risk assessment not only helps identify risks, but prioritizes them so the institution can determine which risks should be measured and controlled based on its business model.

Like a panel of judges, the job of a risk assessor is to evaluate the institution's level of risk by measuring and scoring two key forms of risk: inherent risk and residual risk.

INHERENT RISK

Inherent risk scores represent the level of risk an institution would face if there weren't controls to mitigate it. For example, think of the risk of a cyberattack if the institution didn't have any defenses in place.

One way to look at inherent risk is through the following formula:

Inherent risk = Impact of an event * Probability

This formula demonstrates the relationship between an event's impact and its probability when determining inherent risk. The impact is an estimate of the harm that could be caused by the risk. For example, a cyber breach could have a catastrophic impact. Probability is how likely a risk is to occur. For example, a cyber breach seems a very likely occurrence when there's no firewalls, anti-virus software, or intrusion detection software to prevent it.

Gauging risk in the absence of any controls is a very subjective task, which makes it necessary to have guidelines in place to help assessors understand what defines risk categories and how to label them. For example, guidelines might suggest that frequency of audit findings is a good indicator of probability. An audit finding (or repeat findings) from the past year may indicate a risk is highly likely/probable while one from five years ago with no repeat findings may indicate an unlikely or remote risk. Industry benchmarks, peer experience, economic trends, key ratios, multi-year comparisons of data, board minutes, and media reports can also help inform assessments.

The overly cautious might be tempted to label every risk a significant or high risk, but that's a terrible idea. In a world with limited audit resources, it's incumbent on assessors to provide information about where to best spend those resources. If every risk is labeled high risk, the board won't know where to deploy resources. Higher-risk areas should be addressed more frequently and their control effectiveness reviewed more aggressively. That can't be done if every risk is a labeled a high risk.

RESIDUAL RISK

Residual risk is the risk that remains after controls are taken into account. In the case of a cyber breach, it's the risk that remains after considering deterrence measures. This score helps the organization review its risk tolerance against its strategic objectives. It's all about understanding the relationship between risk and controls. This relationship can be demonstrated with the following formula:

Residual risk = Inherent risk * Control effectiveness

Residual risk is greatest when the inherent risk is high and the controls for mitigating the risk aren't effective. It decreases when controls are effective.

That makes it important to have a method for determining how effective individual controls are. (We'll discuss control weighing, or how effective a control is compared to other controls in just a bit.) This comes down to two factors: the impact of the control and how likely it is to work. This relationship can be expressed with the following formula:

Control effectiveness = Control impact * % Effective

A control's impact is the expected value of its risk mitigation. A control can be viewed as very important, important, or not very important. For example, a firewall can be very important for keeping out hackers because it covers the entire institution. A control's effectiveness is the probability that the control will function as intended based on assessments. When it comes to firewalls, monitoring reports can show evidence of the firewall fending off specific attacks, but it may also indicate that occasionally a new attack has made some inroads. When assessing effectiveness, make sure controls are regularly monitored for trends to help understand if they are performing as expected. (We'll dig deeper into this later on.)

Risk Is Relative

Free soloing, if you're unfamiliar with the term, is climbing without a rope, safety gear, or a climbing partner. It was the subject of the 2019 Oscar-winning documentary Free Solo, which followed Alex Honnold's journey to become the first person to ever free solo climb El Capitan, the 3,000-foot-tall rock formation in Yosemite National Park.

The tiniest mistake, like a loose rock or being startled by a bird, could have caused Honnold to fall to his death. Even the film crew of climbers documenting Alex's attempt could barely watch for fear that their friend might not survive.

What makes someone take on this kind of risk? A functional MRI revealed that Honnold's amygdala, the section of the brain that processes emotions including fear, requires a much higher level of stimuli to activate fear than the average person.

He looks at risk with a level of dispassion most people are incapable of. As he puts it:

"I like to differentiate between risk and consequence. You know, when I'm doing these hard free solos I'd like to think that the risk, the chance of me falling off, is quite low even though the consequence is extremely high."

For a risk averse banker, this feels like an insane way to gauge risk.

We measure inherent risk by considering the probability of an event and the severity of its impact. And while the likelihood of Honnold falling is low (I'll take his word for that, though I saw him have two mishaps during the documentary), the impact is severe. We can even calculate the severity of the impact: 9.8 meters per second until he hits the ground, according to my old friend gravity.

Alex may feel like the low probability is enough to counter the severe impact, but that's not the way I see it.

As a friend and climbing partner of Honnold explains, "There's no margin for error. Imagine an Olympic-gold-medal-level athletic achievement that if you don't get that gold medal, you're going to die."

Perhaps Honnold considers the risk of falling low because he is assessing residual risk, or the risk that remains after controls are taken into account.

Honnold may not have a rope or a helmet, but he does have a plan and plenty of experience. In addition to free soloing other rocks, he's spent years planning and climbing El Capitan with ropes. He's made note of every foothold and handhold in a climbing journal and carefully detailed his route down to the centimeter.

This mental and physical preparation has given Honnold confidence that the risk is low, and yet even his friends seem to disagree. "People who know a little bit about mountain climbing think oh, he's totally safe," notes a climbing partner. "People who really know exactly what's he's doing are freaked out."

They have reason to be. There is a long list of free solo climbers who've fallen to their death, including a renowned Swiss free solo climber who fell over half a mile to his death in the Himalayas in 2017—just a month before Alex attempted El Capitan.

It makes me wonder how effective Hannold's controls really are.

It's also a reminder that risk assessments vary from person to person and that everyone has a different risk appetite. One person's insane gambit is another person's undeniable quest.

When determining impact and probability for risks and controls, draw on the background information gathered and address the issue with an open mind. Consider the risk of a fire. A fire can have a huge impact, but many don't consider it a high risk because it may seem unlikely. Often that's because they've never experienced a fire or don't know anyone who has. Fires seem like rare events.

However, these individuals are failing to properly consider the inherent risk: the risk in the absence of controls. The reason there are relatively few building fires is that the modern world has many tools to prevent fires. We don't heat our homes with open flames or use oil lamps and candles for lighting. There are building and electrical codes, sprinkler systems, and fire-resistant building materials. Take those controls away and fires become more common. This is an example where personal experience may cloud practical judgement. Fire is an inherently high risk.

Now let's look at controls. There are multiple controls to mitigate the inherent risk of a fire, including fire extinguishers, sprinkler systems, smoke detectors, alarm systems, etc. While these can all be valuable controls, they are not equal. Different controls work better in different situations, and some are just more effective at mitigating risk than others.

For instance, a fire extinguisher has a lower expected risk mitigation value than a sprinkler system. It simply isn't of much value in the event of a large-scale fire. Therefore, if an institution doesn't have as many working fire extinguishers as it should, but its sprinkler system is operational, the fact that its fire extinguishers aren't 100 percent effective won't necessarily have a dramatic impact on the residual risk. Conversely, if there are plenty of operable fire extinguishers but the sprinkler system isn't working properly or consistently, then the residual risk would be affected because the sprinkler system is a more impactful control.

The same control can have a high impact score in one situation and a low impact score in another. The difference is the situation in which it is used. For example, a handheld fire extinguisher is great for a small, contained fire, but not particularly helpful if the building is already engulfed in frames. When determining the impact rating, assume that the control is being used for its intended purpose. Also think about how a control can fall short. A handheld fire extinguisher won't work unless someone knows where the fire extinguisher is and how to operate it. The extinguisher must be fully charged. If any of these items is missing, the probability that particular control will be effective is lowered.

A fire is a common example used in risk management, but let's apply this logic to something a little more relatable to the banking industry: collecting data for the Customer Identification Program (CIP) provisions of the USA PATRIOT Act. The PATRIOT Act requires that an institution collect five key pieces of customer information before opening an account. A review of enforcement actions related to anti-money laundering violations indicates there is a significant inherent risk in failing to fill this requirement.

This risk can be reduced with several controls. They include:

- Automated software that prevents an account opening from moving forward without the information
- A checklist for employees
- Quality control by double checking a sample of new accounts

On the surface, these all seems like great controls, but assessments over time can demonstrate the strengths and weaknesses of each control.

The automated software ensures that information is entered 100 percent of the time. No fields are left blank. However, it can't guarantee the correct information is entered. The checklist has potential for human error and an audit may demonstrate that employees often skip this step. Finally, an assessment of quality control may show that the process is extremely effective in ensuring the proper information is entered, but it's only used on a sampling of new accounts because it's too time consuming to do for each new account.

The fact that the institution is inconsistent on the checklist, a relatively unimportant control, probably won't have a huge impact on the institution's overall residual risk. It might even decide to discontinue this control due to its ineffectiveness. It all comes down to risk tolerance and effectiveness. If after assessing its controls, it decides the residual risk is too high, it can introduce new controls or dedicate more resources to existing ones.

That's why it's important to look internally when it comes to scoring controls. While an institution should draw from peer institutions' experience when thinking about potential risks, control scores must be specific to the institution being assessed. This is one instance where it doesn't matter what the institution down the street is doing.

RISK AND CONTROL SCORING

Interviewing a department isn't an ideal method for assessing risk. Interviews produce qualitative data. This is non-numerical data based on observations and experiences. While this information is valuable for risk discussions and background, when it comes to measuring risk for assessments, this subjective data won't be of much value to your institution or your regulators.

Quantitative data, or data that can be expressed with numbers, is much more valuable when making risk determinations. Examples include the number of high-risk customers, the dollar amount of foreign wires in a given time period, or financial losses due to fraud.

To compare risks and controls, it's necessary to have a scoring system. The way that scale is structured can influence risk and control scores. Some institutions use a three-point scale of high, medium, and low. Others use a five-point scale since it offers more nuance. For example, risk can be rated on a scale from 1 to 5 with 1 representing a low risk and 5 representing the highest possible level of risk. Others use terms like catastrophic, significant, moderate, minor, and insignificant. Similarly, controls can be ranked on a scale of 1 to 5 with 1 representing controls that do the least to reduce risk and 5 representing those that are the most effective. Others use terms to assess the probability that a control will be effective. These can include "certain," "likely," "possible," "unlikely," and "remote."

The scoring of risks and controls can be time consuming, especially when the process turns into scoring debates. If this happens, change gears to make sure those debating the scores have a similar understanding of the risk or control. Time spent on education pays far larger dividends than debates on individual scores. Instinctive reactions are far more likely to be accurate when assessors share a common knowledge base. Without that knowledge, they are just guessing, and risk assessments will not be consistent.

RISK TREATMENT

Once risks are identified and assessed, an institution needs to be sure it understands those risks. It should consider a variety of options for mitigating them and settle on a plan. That plan should identify risk owners, typically departments or business processes. There also needs to be a risk manager tasked with remediation of any residual risk items in excess of pre-defined risk tolerance and implementation under a specific timeframe. The institution should also think about establishing an early warning system using key risk indicators (KRIs) and other regulatory monitored ratios or data, so it is aware when risks are evolving. This information makes it possible to make timely adjustments to strategic goals and objectives if needed.

MONITORING AND REVIEW

Once risks are known and understood, they must be monitored and reviewed. The institution should have thresholds in place and a plan for acting on new information. For example, if the institution has a KRI early warning system, there should be policies and procedures in place for determining when action is necessary and when a wait-and-see approach is appropriate.

Change is inevitable and an institution needs to decide when it will update its risk assessment. Will it update the risk assessment on an as-needed basis or on a periodic frequency? To properly manage risk, updates should be made in as close to real time as possible.

A timely response to all risk assessment and remediation efforts is essential. Management and the board need all the relevant information so that they can study both the risks and the opportunities.

COMMUNICATION

An institution can have the most carefully thought-out risk assessments and intricately crafted risk tolerances, but if they aren't communicated throughout the institution, they are almost worthless. Risk management must be part of the institution's culture. Otherwise, it's just going through the motions.

Training shouldn't just tell people what they should and shouldn't do. It should explain the reasoning for why activities are encouraged or prohibited so that employees learn how to manage risk.

Information about risk needs to be communicated in an accurate and timely manner to be useful. It must travel in many directions. Strategy and risk tolerances should be communicated down from the board. Frontline staff and other employees need to share information upwards to management about new, emerging, and changing risks. Management needs to send information to the board and also down to staff. This should all be documented with policies and procedures. Board portals and employee facing intranet sites can be helpful communication tools.

The need to communicate about risk management can be emphasized with training, but only if it is presented the right way. Training shouldn't just tell people what they should and shouldn't do. It should explain the reasoning for why activities are encouraged or prohibited so that employees learn how to manage risk. Consistent communication is essential and should hold up successes just as often as it highlights failures.

DEFINING RISK METRICS

Risk indicators are early warning signs. They help an institution recognize changes in risk conditions, allowing management to take mitigating action to ensure the institution continually operates within its defined risk tolerance.

When it comes to risk monitoring, there are two main types of indicators: key performance indicators (KPIs) and key risk indicators (KRIs).

KPIs monitor the achievement of important objectives that represent the institution's health. They track known issues by helping institutions define and measure progress towards established goals and objectives. They evaluate the success of past performance, revealing performance issues and potential risks. Examples include:

- Sales revenue growth
- Customer service resolution times
- Website traffic
- Customer retention

KPIs get a lot of attention because they are obvious measures of actively pursued goals. They offer a higher-level view of organizational, line of business, or departmental trends or performance. But risk management isn't just about reaching existing goals—it's about uncovering emerging risks. That's where KRIs come in.

KRIs are forward-looking predictors of important measures representing risk. In short, they provide early warning signs of potential problems— ones an institution doesn't even realize it has yet. Examples include:

- High percentage of first payment default loans
- Frequent turnover of key personnel
- High rate of customer complaints
- Upward trend of virus penetrations to systems

KRIs help an institution understand and evaluate risk levels across the organization, a line of business, or a department. These ratios help track and trend evolving risks, potential weaknesses, and opportunities. They signal a need for action and an explanation.

KRIs are extremely valuable—but only if used properly. Glancing at one month or quarter's KRIs might reveal a problem, but it's far more revealing to examine KRIs from a historical perspective to find worrisome trends.

Consider employee turnover. If employees are leaving an institution month after month, it can become a major, costly problem. Not only does churn cause the institution to incur the cost of replacing employees, but a newer or less talented workforce can increase error rates or change the way the institution does business. Monitoring turnover trends can help the institution investigate why people are leaving and solve the problem.

Similarly, first payment defaults can impact the institution's ability to sell loans and maintain liquidity—a significant risk. When an institution sees a steady increase in these defaults, it's a sign that something is not right.

An institution needs a combination of both experience and exposure KRIs. These allow an institution to understand inherent risk and residual risk.

Lagging, leading, and current KRIs are ideal tools for this assessment.

Lagging or current KRIs are also known as experience KRIs. These look backward instead of toward the future. They can be effective in revealing events that may have initially been hidden from view. An example might include the number of errors as a percentage of total transactions. In other words, they aren't obvious until you combine the factors.

A current KRI reflects a point-in-time change in the level of exposure to the applicable risk. Current KRIs are typically those relating to "real time" monitoring of performance, for example system downtime or system capacity usage. A lagging KRI reflects the level of exposure to the applicable risk that has already occurred (e.g., operational losses.)

Leading or exposure KRIs are forward-looking in nature and allow an institution to proactively identify a situation of heightened risk. They are predictive in nature. A loss may not have been experienced yet, but the change in the metric over time may indicate a higher level of exposure to risk. Examples include rising interest rates on potential credit issues or policy exceptions on accounts opened without enhanced due diligence.

CHOOSING QUALITY METRICS

There's no shortage of potential metrics, but an institution has only so much time and resources for measuring, monitoring, and reviewing them. An institution needs to carefully select its metrics so that they effectively and efficiently represent key risk drivers. They should be tied to business goals, objectives, and standards and reflect the risk categories the institution faces.

Good metrics should simplify risk without being simplistic. They should be objective and easy to understand, not vague or subjective. They should be developed using consistent methodologies and standards so that everyone throughout the institution understands how they are measured and what the results mean. They should be easy to communicate.

One way to gauge metrics is to determine if they are SMART. Smart stands for:

S	SUSTAINABLE	Cost effective to collect; repeatable
M	MEASURABLE	Quantifiable (percent, ratio, amount, or count); able to be benchmarked internally and/or externally
A	ACTIONABLE	Guides decision-making and management action
R	RELEVANT	Clearly aligned to the risk
T	TIMELY	Consistently measured over time to recognize trends before breaking standards or limits.

ESTABLISHING THRESHOLDS

Risk indicators are a valuable tool, but they require context to be truly valuable. That's why it's essential to set thresholds for each indicator so that it's clear whether the risk level faced by the institution is acceptable (green), requires intervention (yellow) or demands immediate management action (red).

Every institution will have different thresholds depending on factors such as its risk appetite, risk capacity, velocity of risk, customer impact, seasonality, industry benchmarks, employee experience, historical data, forward-looking data (such as new controls and growth), and forecasts or budgets.

It's common for risk indicators to fluctuate over time. In fact, it's a good thing. If an institution's risk indicators are always green, the thresholds might be too broad, the indicator might not be measuring a key risk, or it's a poor indicator of risk. Consistently red indicators present a problem of their own. If an indicator is constantly red, it might be a false alarm or may need to be re-evaluated to see if it's really a problem.

Selecting thresholds is not an arbitrary exercise and it should not be done casually. As with the risk indicators they quantify, thresholds should be approved by the appropriate level of management to ensure buy in. There also needs to be an escalation protocol for when thresholds are breached.

THE DANGER OF SKIPPING OVER KRIs AND KPIs

Just 30 percent of internal audit departments in the U.S. regularly identify and monitor key risk indicators (KRIs), including those that suggest growing or emerging risks, according to the 2019 North American Pulse of Internal Audit survey from the Institute of Internal Auditors. Twenty three percent of the 500 companies surveyed don't use them at all.[73]

This is a huge oversight. KRIs and KPIs are an important part of corporate governance and risk management, helping shape strategic goals and risk appetite. Without information on performance, the board and management have no way of measuring the success of a program or making truly informed decisions.

There are many reasons why management may be slow to adopt strategic planning, enterprise risk management, and key indicators to track progress. They include:

Desire for perfection. With the operating environment constantly evolving, some financial institutions don't want to waste time detailing a strategic plan or risk appetite that might change. This is a mistake. Successful institutions regularly adjust their strategic plans. In fact, they are more nimble in responding because they have indicators to track their progress.

They don't want to highlight failures. If you don't outline expectations, you can't fall short of them. This lack of transparency results in poor governance. Understanding issues from a business management perspective should never be seen as negative.

Lack of confidence in the data. If an institution suspects its data is inaccurate or it doesn't have data that aligns with what needs to be measured, it may not bother with KPIs. Yet risk and opportunity are only identifiable through adoption of a consistent process.

Fear of finding too many risks. Indicators may contradict gut feelings, and management doesn't want to concede the possibility that they are wrong. Yet there is no way of knowing what the results are without measurements. Risk may be rising, but it also could be level or even declining.

Limited experience in performing ongoing success and risk monitoring. Management isn't really sure how to accomplish this task, so they just skip it.

When setting strategic objectives, KPIs should help understand whether those goals are being met within the expected risk tolerance. They may identify:

- **Risk occurring at a higher frequency than expected.** This may impact the understood likelihood of risk and may negatively impact the defined residual risk.
- **Risk occurring at a much lower frequency than expected.** This may impact the understood likelihood of risk and may positively impact the defined residual risk.

- **Expectations not being met.** This may warrant a change in the risk appetite, either allowing more risk or less.
- **Expectations exceeded.** This may mean that an institution should consider a greater allowance of risk to explore opportunities fully.

Imagine a financial institution that wants to increase its digital footprint. There are plenty of ways to measure both success and risks. Success can be gauged by member/customer usage and penetration, the number of new accounts opened, or an increase in fee income. Risk can be gauged by financial loss, complaints, and internal costs including labor.

These indicators should be regularly monitored with milestones along the way. This keeps the board and senior management focused on whether the institution is achieving the strategic plan's established goals. This includes whether timelines and objectives are being met and if additional or alternative actions need to be implemented. For example, if the institution's risk appetite for financial loss on an initiative is $100,000, management shouldn't wait until that threshold is met to inform the board. It should set triggers for key milestones along the way, such as $20,000, $40,000, and $60,000, so the board can stay apprised.

When these key risk indicators are triggered, it gives the board and management an opportunity to investigate what's going wrong. This may include a risk vs. reward analysis, a study of the control environment, or a wait-and-see approach to ascertain if it's the result of a one-off or something more systematic.

Failing to monitor indicators can lead to regulatory scrutiny. It also limits an institution's ability to be proactive, instead fostering a reactive environment, which limits its ability to be agile and quickly recover from failure.

The road to strategic success is paved with good intentions. Failing to track risk and performance can lead to a rocky detour.

THE TRUTH ABOUT ASSET-BASED RISK ASSESSMENTS

Wouldn't it be nice to reduce risk management to a simple checklist? You could go down a list of business assets, answer a few questions, and be on your way.

That's the thinking behind asset-based risk management, a buzzy risk management catchphrase. Unfortunately, this idea has more flash than substance and could lead a financial institution to overlook or underestimate risks, exposing the institution to unwanted risk and creating the potential for noncompliance with regulatory expectations.

An asset-based risk assessment examines risk by reviewing an institution's assets. Asset-based risk assessments are most closely associated with IT, information security, and Gramm-Leach-Bliley Act (GLBA) and data privacy since on the surface these areas seem most closely tied to physical assets.

When it comes to IT security, the FFIEC Information Security Handbook defines assets as "hardware, software, information, and connections."[74] This may include major applications, general support systems, high-impact programs, physical plant, mission-critical systems, personnel, equipment, or a logically related group of systems.

An asset-based risk assessment begins with a list of assets. Each listed asset is individually reviewed to determine potential threats and vulnerabilities as well as the effectiveness of existing controls. The result is a long list of threats and controls by asset.

The problem with asset-based assessments isn't what it includes—it's what it leaves out.

The FFIEC IT Examination Handbook - Appendix A: Examination Procedures[75] lists examination objectives that tell a financial institution everything that will be within an examiner's scope during an IT exam, including the area of risk management. Unfortunately, an asset-based risk assessment doesn't touch many of these areas.

Asset-based risk assessments don't consider things like:

- Policies and procedures
- Board management and oversight
- Governance
- Reporting
- Board training and experience
- Risk management processes

Yet these areas are clearly within the scope of an IT exam as defined by the FFIEC's listed objectives. Consider the following objectives listed in Appendix A and how an asset-based risk assessment would fail to address them.

Objective 2: Determine whether the board oversees and senior management appropriately establishes an effective governance structure that includes oversight of IT activities.

Problem: If your institution is relying on asset-based risk management, the governance structure will be overlooked, and the risks here will not be measured.

Objective 6: Evaluate management's review and oversight of IT controls, including the other influencing functions of IT audit and compliance.

Problem: When looking at personnel and assets, compliance and risk management won't be listed as an asset since neither is likely to be part of the IT department. It's not enough to look at the individual controls protecting an asset. It's important to understand the policies and procedures for reviewing and overseeing these controls.

Objective 7: Determine whether the institution's risk management program facilitates effective risk identification and measurement and provides support for risk decisions within ITRM.

Problem: An asset-based risk management program isn't going to evaluate IT's risk management program because it's not included in the list of assets. It won't address the risk of failing to demonstrate to examiners how management uses information from the risk assessment to make strategic decisions.

Another major problem with asset-based assessments is missing the opportunity to identify functional interdependencies. When you assess risks by asset, you are looking at one small piece of a big enterprise. How are you going to tie it all together? The answer is that you won't.

That means you may be unable to demonstrate to examiners that you have addressed these objectives:

Objective 3: As part of the ITRM structure, determine whether financial institution management has defined IT responsibilities and functions.

Verify the existence of well-defined responsibilities and expectations between risk management and IT functional areas, such as information security, project management, business continuity, and information systems reporting.

Problem: IT doesn't operate in a bubble. It supports functions throughout an institution. An asset-based risk assessment looks at individual assets instead of addressing the interconnected relationship between functional areas.

Objective 4: Determine the adequacy of the institution's IT operations planning and investment. Assess the adequacy of the risk assessment and the overall alignment with the institution's business strategy, including planning for IT resources and budgeting.

Problem: An asset-based risk assessment doesn't consider the risk of failing to align IT planning and risk assessments with the institution's overall strategic goals. Yet examiners will look for it.

Objective 10: Determine whether the institution maintains a risk identification process that is coordinated and consistent across the enterprise.

Objective 11: Determine whether institution management maintains a risk measurement process that is coordinated and consistent across the enterprise.

Problem: Objectives aren't limited to just what goes on in IT. It also looks at the whole program. An asset-based risk assessment won't provide evidence that the institution has a coordinated risk management program.

These are just a few examples of where asset-based assessments can fall short of regulatory expectations. An asset-based risk management program isn't designed to connect the dots in a way that supports ERM. It examines the risks presented by assets like laptops or a building. It doesn't analyze risk by function, and it has no way to measure the expertise of the board.

While the FFIEC guidance specifically mentions asset-based risk assessments, saying that "Management should maintain inventories of assets (e.g., hardware, software, and information), event classes (e.g., natural disaster, cyber, and insider abuse or compromise), threats (e.g., theft, malware, and social engineering), and existing controls as an important part of effective risk identification,"[76] it's important to pay attention to the language.

Note it says, *"part* of effective risk identification." It's not the only tool needed. A list of assets is helpful in identifying those that store or transmit protected data and ensuring there are proper controls in place to mitigate cyber risk. But there is more to risk identification than assets.

Also, risk identification is just one step of the risk management lifecycle. Risks must also be analyzed, mitigated, and monitored. That analysis needs to tie into a system that evaluates risk holistically, providing insights that allow the board and management to make more intelligent decisions that support the institution's strategic goals while fending off threats and maximizing opportunities.

Asset-based assessments just don't do that.

Risk identification is just one step of the risk management lifecycle. Risks must also be analyzed, mitigated, and monitored.

GOVERNING RISK MEASUREMENT AND REPORTING

The board is ultimately responsible for governance and oversight, but management and other personnel play an important role in reporting on risk measurement outcomes. There needs to be a structure in place to create accountability for measuring and reporting risk so that the board has timely and accurate information to make decisions. Residual risks in excess of tolerance should be reported in a way that is actionable for management yet meaningful to the board.

Different people across the institution will likely be responsible for measuring and monitoring risk. Any given risk measurement is likely to provide information on a variety of risk categories, making it important that everyone understands who is responsible for measuring each specific KRI to avoid duplicate work and inconsistent results. That's why it's a best practice to use a responsibility assignment matrix (RACI) chart to ensure that roles and responsibilities are carefully defined. Personnel should know whom they report to and why and when an issue should be escalated.

It's also important to understand how risk measurements are made. While every institution does its best to develop measurements that accurately reflect real-world conditions, there are times when those measurements are flawed. If indicators don't jive with other measurements, it's important to be able to examine where the results are coming from and investigate whether they are properly reflecting true conditions.

Risk involves many components, making data aggregation a valuable tool. While metrics should be chosen for their value in measuring specific areas, some will naturally be more important than others. When institutions aggregate results with key risk indicator reports, it's essential to establish weights to make it clear where priorities are.

The board needs regular reports on key risk indicator findings to help them execute its risk management responsibilities. With so many findings, it's essential for the board to have access to the most relevant information about risk management, including the areas where it is most actively engaged. Depending on the area of risk, it may include both individual and aggregate findings. Most important, information should be reported with an eye towards providing the most appropriate data for helping the board accomplish its mission. After all, the institution will calculate large amounts of data. The board is likely to need mostly the big picture essentials.

It's not just a question of practicality for business' sake. Regulators are also very interested in knowing the board has reviewed results and whether metrics mesh with corporate objectives. Transparency with them and other third parties is essential.

Thought should go into risk indicator reporting. For instance, elements of key risk indicators should be easily identifiable and data should be trended over an appropriate time period. That can be monthly, quarterly, or some other period, depending on the measure. KRI thresholds and breaches should be clearly identified on any KRI report. There should be no doubt in the reader's mind that a threshold was breached. Readers should also be able to identify which risk categories a KRI aligns with.

FOUR COMMON RISK MONITORING MISTAKES

Financial institutions usually feel confident about enterprise risk management. They've identified and assessed potential risks. Risk tolerance levels have been defined. Strategies are in place for mitigating risk. Yet too often their risk monitoring activities fall short.

Unfortunately, many institutions get monitoring wrong. From missing essential steps to monitoring the wrong things, poor risk monitoring can cause institutions to under or overestimate risk exposure—causing them to make critical decisions based on inaccurate information.

Here are four of the most common risk monitoring mistakes.

1. **Sporadic monitoring.** Risk assessment and monitoring are often checklist activities—institutions decide they should be reviewed once a year or quarter or month and that's when it gets done. No one worries about it again until the next deadline approaches.

   The problem is that a lot can happen in between reviews. Think of cybersecurity. An institution could look at today's data and sees that all is well—never knowing it recently fought off several cyber attacks. The institution might conclude that cyber threats aren't a problem and fail to dedicate resources to improving IT security.

   Just like cybersecurity, risk management requires continuous, ongoing monitoring of risks and internal controls. This gives an institution a clear picture of how risks are changing and lets it adapt its plans accordingly. Otherwise, an institution may have no idea of what new risks are emerging and how exposed it is.

2. **Piggybacking on someone else's standards.** It would save time if institutions could download a master list of risk indicators, but every institution has different needs based on its size, complexity, business activities, location, and other factors. Institutions that use a generic list of industry standards aren't saving time—they are likely wasting time pursuing risks that aren't relevant or ignoring those that are.

   Consider an East Coast bank. It probably doesn't need to invest much time worrying about a potential earthquake. The cost of monitoring the bank's earthquake preparation activities isn't worth the benefit.

The same is true of service or product-related risks. If an institution doesn't offer a product or service, there might be items on a generic list that just don't apply. Monitoring these areas is a waste of resources.

3. **Inconsistent measurements.** Risk management is often siloed. IT handles IT risk assessments, human resources handles HR risk assessments, and each department uses their own methodology and terminology.

    This is a problem. For example, the team handling liquidity risk assessment might use one rating and scoring methodology while the team performing interest rate risk assessment uses another. When it comes time to look at the big picture, those two assessments can't be easily compared because they aren't built on the same foundation. Either the work must be redone or the institution will make a decision based on an inaccurate comparison.

    Institutions can avoid this problem with a standardized approach to monitoring risk that ensures the consistent reporting of information. The whole institution should use the same method to rate risk, assess controls, and set tolerance levels. This way the institution can accurately compare and contrast data to make prudent decisions.

4. **Manual monitoring.** Just like silos make risk monitoring inconsistent, manual processes can make risk monitoring inefficient and inaccurate. When FIs track monitoring across a variety of spreadsheets and file formats in different locations, departments, and branches, something is likely to fall through the cracks. No one can see the big picture. There is no way to know when items are updated or who updated them.

    Manual monitoring makes risk monitoring a passive process where employees must remember to take action instead of an active process where there are notifications, processes, and logs to ensure risks are properly monitored. It's not efficient or effective from an enterprise-wide perspective.

Each of these mistakes minimizes the effectiveness of an institution's risk monitoring program. Ongoing, continuous risk monitoring that measures the right things the right way is essential for facilitating ERM efforts.

Otherwise, the biggest risk might be a failure to properly monitor risk.

CREATING RELIABLE RISK ASSESSMENTS

Risk assessments are only valuable when they are performed correctly. Inconsistent and unreliable risk assessments can cause an institution to make poor decisions by providing inaccurate information. This happens when:

- Risk assessment processes aren't consistent across the organization, leading to varying definitions of risk in each department and more potential risk exposure.
- Employees fail to identify potential risks because they are afraid it will reflect negatively on their performance.
- Employees don't know what the parameters are.
- There is no ongoing process or reliable checkup to ensure that risk controls are valid throughout the risk lifecycle.

CONSISTENCY MATTERS

In a simple world, one person or department would be responsible for conducting every risk assessment. The same approach would be used each time, ensuring consistency.

Unfortunately, nothing is ever simple. At the typical institution, management reviews the results from a variety of risk assessments from every corner of the organization. That makes a consistent approach to the preparation and reporting of risk assessments absolutely essential. This includes:

- **Similar approach and methodology.** While risk assessments are subjective, everyone working on a risk assessment should be aware of how others in the organization are approaching their assessments and the form that those assessments take.
- **Risk and control scores.** The same scales with the same meaning should be used across the institution. A moderate risk rating should have the same meaning for all of the organization's assessments.
- **Formulas for calculating initial and residual risks.** These should be consistent in every risk assessment.

- **Use of inherent and residual risks.** These should be consistent throughout the various risk assessments. It may seem obvious, but there are institutions where one risk assessment considers only residual risk while another assessment in the same organization only considers inherent risks.

Risk assessment consistency isn't just a lofty ideal. It has practical value. Consistency allows for easier comparison and provides a common language for understanding what the results of each risk assessment means. It allows risk assessments to build off each other, facilitating meaningful year-over-year comparisons and department-to-department comparisons that help gauge changes in inherent or residual risks. It ultimately allows the institution to better align strategic objectives and attain goals.

OPTIMISM BIAS: THE ENEMY OF OBJECTIVITY AND CONSISTENCY

Every person brings their own background and experiences, and those influence their risk assessment decisions. While these experiences can bring valuable insights, they can also distort the evaluation of risk. One of the most common problems is a phenomenon known as optimism bias.

Optimism bias, also known as unrealistic or comparative optimism bias, is a person's belief that they are less likely to experience a negative event compared to others. As we talked about earlier, when it comes to the risk of a fire, people might think it's unlikely because they haven't experienced one before, haven't experienced one in this location, or haven't seen or heard of many fires from friends or news reports. These may be accurate and logical statements, but these perceptions are also distorting risk scores. A fire can happen to anyone.

Optimism bias can creep into a risk assessment whether it's performed by a single person or a group of people. Being aware of the existence of potential biases can go a long way towards minimizing their impact. Common forms of optimism bias to be aware of include:

- **Rule of thumb.** We think bad things happen to other organizations because they don't follow the rules. We tell ourselves that since we follow the rules, we have less risk.

- **Loss-aversion bias.** We feel the pain of a loss as much as two times more than the happiness of a gain. That means when weighing risk, we're more likely to focus on the risk of loss than potential gains, even when the gains are likely to outweigh the risks. Similarly, we see the harm in a price increase more than we see the benefit of a price decrease.

- **Overconfidence bias.** This occurs when we believe that our knowledge, skills, or experiences give us an edge in decision making that others don't have. It causes us to place unearned value in our own ideas instead of systematically assessing the validity of others' suggestions.

- **Endowment bias.** We have a natural tendency to place greater value in the things we own. For example, a bank board might refuse a market-value offer to buy the bank because they believe the bank's value was underestimated—but they can't offer any financially sound reasons for why it should be worth more.

- **Status quo bias.** Given the choice between change and keeping things the way they are, it's common for people to prefer to keep things as they are. It's avoiding change even when the risk of doing nothing is greater than the risk of taking action.

- **Singular focus.** It's natural that we know more about our organization than we do about others. Since those firsthand experiences feel more real, we tend to generalize when it comes to others and focus on our own feelings and experiences. This can cause us to neglect the reality of the average organization. This singular focus on self can be avoided by actively working to take a broad view of risks and thinking globally.

- **Interpersonal distance.** Perceived risk differences depend on how far or close any particular risk is to the individual making the risk determination. The further the distance, the more vagueness gets introduced into the determination process. Read up on peer institutions that have dealt with situations to remind your team that your organization is not immune to their problems.

- **Confirmation bias.** This is when risk assessors are influenced by the goals of the organization. The result is that the assessor sees what they want to see instead of the actual risks. Make sure assessors know they won't be penalized for honesty.

Optimism bias can also affect control scores. It's perfectly natural for us to feel that we have more control over situations than we might realistically expect. Sometimes that perceived control is real. Other times it's not. Imagine a passenger riding with a friend who just bought a brand-new sports car. The passenger is gripping the dashboard with white knuckles and begging their friend to slow down while zipping down on a windy road. The driver responds by praising the car's superb handling. The difference here is perspective. The passenger doesn't have any control over the situation. The driver is impressed by how well the car handles curves and the gas pedal's responsiveness. If the driver and passenger were to stop and switch positions, the tables may turn.

When assessing controls, consider the viewpoint of both the proverbial driver and the passenger. The truth is probably somewhere in between.

Emotional bias in risk assessments and decision making is insidious, but it's not unavoidable. Emotional bias is based more on snap judgments than careful reasoning. While our gut decisions can offer insight, they should be complemented with an assessment of available data. It's helpful to act as a devil's advocate to look for flaws in your assessments. Invite others to pick it apart and be open to their suggestions. It also helps to slow down. Emotional bias is a crutch when you're under pressure to make a prompt decision. It's cheaper and easier to add a few days or weeks to the decision process than it is to undo a bad decision down the road.

AVOIDING COMMON MISTAKES

When conducting a risk assessment, the role of the assessors is to rate risks and controls as accurately as possible. Some people make the mistake of confusing a risk assessment with a job performance review. They don't want to give a bad grade so they err on the side of optimism. Assessors must be reminded that their job isn't to push for organizational objectives or to make people look good. The job is to form as complete a risk picture as possible so the institution can make smarter, more informed decisions.

*It can't be said enough:
risk assessments are not performance reviews.*

The role of a risk assessor is not to fulfill the goals or desires of the organization. That denies management the opportunity to be aware of issues and take appropriate steps to accept or remediate the risk.

Sometimes, risk assessors want to avoid showing too many "red" rankings and aim for "green" because they fear getting someone in trouble. This is a mistake. It can't be said enough: risk assessments are not performance reviews. Risk is a part of business, and different parts of the organization will have different degrees of risk. Having a high initial or residual risk rating does not necessarily mean that someone is doing a poor job. Just think of cybersecurity. The inherent risk of a breach when there are no controls is extraordinarily high. Pretending it *isn't* won't help the institution make smarter cybersecurity decisions. It will only give it a false sense of security. The same is true of controls and residual risk. Even with controls in place, sometimes risk remains high.

The goal of a risk assessment is not to eliminate risk. It's to align an institution's risk exposure and management with its risk tolerance and goals. The information gleaned from a well-executed risk assessment gives management and the board valuable insights that help it make better decisions that contribute to the safety and soundness of the institution while allowing it to make the most of potential opportunities.

*The goal of a risk assessment is not to eliminate risk.
It's to align an institution's risk exposure and management
with its risk tolerance and goals.*

CHAPTER EIGHT

APPLYING ERM TO BANKING

The key to creating reliable risk assessments is consistency and awareness of potential biases.

I t's no fun to be a cautionary tale. Just ask Target.

I'm sure you remember the mega-retailer's 2013 data security breach. Who could forget? It affected 41 million customer payment card accounts and exposed contact information for more than 60 million customers after hackers entered Target's system through a third-party HVAC vendor and installed malware at its registers to steal data. Target is still held up as the standard example of third-party vendor management gone wrong, even after reaching an $18.5 million breach settlement with 47 states' attorneys general in 2018. (Talk about reputation risk.)

At least Target lived to sell another day, unlike WaMu, Bear Stearns, and the other brands littering the graveyard of the mortgage crisis. They were victims of their failure to take risk seriously.

ARMs weren't a new invention when big banks and mortgage brokers began offering them with reckless abandon during the mortgage boom. They had been available in the U.S. since the late 1970s and had been popular in Europe and Australia years before that. They were designed to help specific customers in specific circumstances and were intended to be provided only after carefully explaining the risks to consumers who typically pictured fixed-rate, 30-year loans when they heard the word mortgage. It's only when mortgage brokers started steering people to inappropriate loans and failing to provide proper income and other documentation that ARMs began to blow up, permanently tainting the product's reputation.

It's tales like this that make many financial institutions wary of new products or services. Bankers don't like surprises. When they hear a horror story, they tend to shut down discussion of whatever it was that went wrong, not wanting to find themselves in the same situation.

However, pretending these instances don't exist is a mistake. From mortgage lending to burgeoning digital technologies like P2P payment portals, there is no shortage of potential opportunities for financial institutions looking to expand business lines and grow profits. The key is to properly manage the risk at the strategic level so that the institution doesn't enter into the activity with blinders on. That knowledge will help an institution develop controls to help mitigate those risks.

Let's take a look at how we can effectively implement controls to manage common risks in the financial services industry.

ANALYZING RISK IN MORTGAGE LENDING

We've already talked about what happened in mortgage lending when risk was taken out of the equation. It wasn't pretty, tanking both the U.S. and the world economy. Now let's explore the right way to analyze risk.

Remember when many institutions were seeing their traditional mortgage line stagnate? With ho-hum rates and strict qualified mortgage guidelines that made mortgages a commodity business, many found it hard to compete. To make up the lost revenue, some institutions may have chosen to enter business lending, receivables financing, or more exotic lending. Or, in the example we're about to examine, an institution may have set a strategic goal of boosting revenue by increasing the amount of mortgage lending it does. But before a decision like this can be made, a thorough mortgage lending risk assessment or review and update of the existing one it necessary.

The assessment begins by identifying the specific risks mortgage lending presents and then classifying the types of risks they represent. This can include operational, transaction, compliance, credit, strategic, reputation, cyber, third-party, and concentration risk.

To give you an idea of the process, let's take a look at compliance risk. Increasing regulatory burden has pushed many community bank and credit union lenders out of the mortgage arena, making compliance risk a critical factor. The list of potential risks includes:

Regulation	Risk
Regulation Z	Proper disclosures for radio, TV, and print advertising
Equal Credit Opportunity Act (ECOA)	Improper handling of joint applicants on applications
Home Mortgage Disclosure Act (HMDA)	Compliance with change in regulation
Fair Lending	Loan officers using different standards to evaluate collateral
	Higher percentage of minority loan applications denied
Secure and Fair Enforcement for Mortgage Licensing Act (SAFE Act)	Failure to add and register new covered staff
Service Members Civil Relief Act of 2003	Not extending SCRA relief to eligible family members
Community Reinvestment Act (CRA)	Not lending to minority or moderate-income neighborhoods
TILA-RESPA Integrated Disclosures (TRID)	Calculation of APRs

IDENTIFYING INHERENT RISK

Once the risks of mortgage lending are known, an institution needs to measure how exposed it would be to each of those risks. To do that, it needs to calculate the inherent risk, or the risk an institution would face if there were no controls in place at the institution to mitigate the risk. As a reminder, the formula for inherent risk is:

Inherent risk = Impact of an event * Probability

When measuring inherent risk, we'll use a 5-point scale. For impact we'll use the terms (in order from most to least severe) catastrophic, significant, moderate, minor, and insignificant to measure risk and its potential impact. Probability will be measured with the terms (in order from most to least likely) certain, likely, possible, unlikely, and remote.

Inherent Risk	Event Impact	Probability
Low (1)	Insignificant (1)	Remote (1)
Moderate-Low (2)	Minor (2)	Unlikely (2)
Moderate (3)	Moderate (3)	Possible (3)
High-Moderate (4)	Significant (4)	Likely (4)
High (5)	Catastrophic (5)	Certain (5)

Consider the risk of failing to make proper disclosures for radio, TV, and print advertising. The consequences for not using the proper disclosures are very serious. Regulators will come down hard on this type of violation, making the event impact significant. The likelihood of not using the proper disclosures is a bit lower. It's not inevitable that the institution will make a mistake, but it's definitely not impossible. A ranking of possible is appropriate.

When we apply the formula, we compare the severity to the likelihood to determine inherent risk. While the consequences for using the wrong disclosures are very severe, when you consider that it's not particularly likely to happen, it lowers the inherent risk of the activity. In this case, the inherent risk appears to be moderate.

IDENTIFYING CONTROLS
TO IDENTIFY RESIDUAL RISK

Next, we need to calculate residual risk. That formula again is:

Residual risk = Inherent risk * Control effectiveness

To do this, we need to understand how effective the institution's controls for preventing the problem are expected to be. We do that with the following formula:

Control effectiveness = Control impact * % Effective

To make this calculation, an institution must identify all the current controls it has in place or determine what controls it would use if it undertook the activity. Examples include policies and procedures, training, audits, or quality control. For instance, to mitigate the risk of failing to add and register new covered staff under the SAFE Act an institution might create a centralized registration with human resources and then register new staff during onboarding, a moderately effective control. To calculate annual percentage interest rate (APRs) under TRID, it might conduct quality control of its software's accuracy. To avoid different loan officers using different standards when evaluating collateral and violating the Equal Credit Opportunity Act, an institution might implement compliance training.

In conducting this exercise, control impact will be measured on a five-point scale (unimportant, minor, moderate, significant, very important). Effectiveness will be measured on a scale of 0 to 100 percent.

Control Effectiveness	Control Impact	% Effective
Low (1)	Very Important (5)	100%
Moderate-Low (2)	Significant (4)	75-99%
Moderate (3)	Moderate (3)	50-75%
High-Moderate (4)	Minor (2)	21-49%
High (5)	Unimportant (1)	1-20%

In the case of advertising disclosures, the biggest control an institution has is its policies and procedures. These controls have a significant impact. They don't absolutely stop all risk, but they don't set the bar low either. The effectiveness comes down to how well the institution will implement the controls, ensuring the policies and procedures are properly executed. With the right tools, this is very possible, though there is always a chance for human error. As such, control effectiveness is 80%.

Comparing the control impact with the control effectiveness (refer to the formula above), I'd rate the control as moderate.

DETERMINING RESIDUAL RISK

Now on to calculating residual risk. Residual risk is the aggregate score for all controls related to a risk. Once all the individual controls have been evaluated and weighed, an institution can calculate the overall effectiveness of a particular risk's controls and compare it to the inherent risk of the activity.

Residual risk = Inherent risk (Moderate) * Control (Moderate)

Put into words, there is a moderate risk with moderate controls. The level of control is appropriate for the level of risk, therefore the residual risk may be ranked as minor.

As you can see, the formula isn't entirely mathematical. It requires a lot of subjective judgements on how likely events are to occur and how effective controls will be. There may be times when an inherent risk score of moderate and a control score of moderate result in a residual risk of minor.

Sample Mortgage Compliance Risk Controls

DEPARTMENT	REGULATION	RISK	Risk Impact	Risk Likelihood	Initial Risk	Residual Risk	CONTROL	Control Impact	Control Likelihood	Control Effectiveness	Raw Residual Risk
Mortgage Lending	Advertising of Products	Improper disclosures for radio, TV and print advertising	5	3	3	1	Policies and Procedures	3	4	3	1
Mortgage Lending	Equal Credit Oppurtunity Act	Improper handling of joint applicants on applications	5	4	4	2	Compliance Audit Training	3	3	3	2
Mortgage Lending	Fair Lending	Loan Officers using different standards to evaluate collateral leading to fair lending violations	4	5	4	2	Collateral is appraised by an independant appraiser	3	3	3	2
Mortgage Lending	Fair Lending	Higher percentage of minority loan applications declined	5	4	4	2	Compliance Audit	3	3	3	2
Mortgage Lending	Fair Lending	Higher percentage of minority loan applications declined	5	4	4	2	Training	3	4	3	2
Mortgage Lending	Fair Lending	Higher percentage of minority loan applications declined	5	4	4	2	Quality Control	4	3	3	2
Mortgage Lending	Home Mortgage Diclosure Act	Noncompliance with change in Regulation	5	3	3	1	Training Staff	3	3	3	1
Mortgage Lending	Home Mortgage Diclosure Act	Noncompliance with change in Regulation	5	3	3	1	Updating Policies and Procedures	3	4	3	1
Mortgage Lending	Secure and Fair Enforcement for Mortgage Licensing Act of 2008	Failure to add and register new covered staff	3	3	3	1	Centralize registration with HR and registration during onboarding	3	3	3	1
Mortgage Lending	Service Members Civil Relief Act of 2003	Not extending SCRA relief to eligible family members	5	4	4	2	Training	3	3	3	2
Mortgage Lending	TRID	Miscalculation of APRs	4	4	4	2	Software Accuracy - Quality Control	3	4	3	2

The information gained from this exercise can be used to make an important decision: is the institution willing to accept the residual risk as presented? Perhaps additional controls are needed to be put in place before it will be comfortable increasing mortgage lending. Maybe it would prefer to outsource. These ideas need to be considered and revised risk assessments run to calculate new residual risk ratings.

It comes down to the institution's risk appetite and whether or not the residual risk presents too much risk for increased mortgage lending to be worth the risk.

The same exercise should be performed across all risk categories. Just imagine if the big banks had thought about credit risk during the mortgage boom instead of assuming it would blow up in someone else's face if something went wrong. They might have realized that it was likely they'd have to buy back loans that failed to meet performance standards, reducing the incentive to write subprime ARMs to customers and then packaging the poorly documented loans to sell to investors. They might have put in stronger controls to ensure those selling mortgages in their name were doing so ethically, following policies and procedures.

In the end, only an individual institution can determine whether the risk is worth the potential reward.

DIGITAL STRATEGIES: ASSESSING THE RISK

Digital banking has become an unstoppable force. As many as, half of adults worldwide use a smartphone, tablet, PC, or smartwatch to access financial services, according to a report by Juniper Research.[77] The struggle financial institutions face is how to ensure that those consumers are choosing to engage with their institution in an increasingly crowded financial services marketplace.

There's no shortage of competition. From traditional FDIC-insured institutions to a bevy of fintech disrupters, there have never been more options available to consumers. The question, then, is to understand what consumers want.

The answer varies according to who you ask. Some studies say ease of use[78] while others say speed.[79] Many argue for simplicity while others argue for customization. Ultimately, the answers all point to one commonality: technology can be a real differentiator for financial institutions.

There are a variety of cutting-edge products on the market, including voice technology, virtual reality, predictive analytics, marketplace lending, and digital wallets like Apple Pay. Deciding which technologies to embrace and when is a strategic decision for any financial institution, one that presents a variety of risks.

In this case, let's stick to the basics and consider some of the risks a financial institution should consider when embarking on a common strategy: increasing customer engagement through mobile and internet banking to capture a larger share of online users and traffic. It may not seem very exciting compared to some emerging technologies, but it presents risks nonetheless.

Potential digital banking risks include:

Cybersecurity. There is no shortage of potential cybersecurity issues. Firewalls can be breached. Personal information can be compromised. Social engineering exploits can cause spyware, malware, or ransomware to be inadvertently installed on the client's or user's machines. And in all these cases, the results can be catastrophic.

Proper disclosures. Every new channel represents another area where disclosures must be posted and regularly updated.

Not knowing the customer. Online customers are subject to the PATRIOT Act's Know Your Customer regulations even though they never step foot in the bank, creating a compliance risk.

Fraud. When a customer walks into an institution it's easy to recognize a face or check identification. Online technologies can present greater risks of fraud, making it harder to verify a customer's identity.

Customer complaint volume. Increased usage will inevitably lead to increased complaints and the institution will need the structure in place to keep pace.

A CLOSER LOOK AT CYBER RISKS

These are all substantial risks. Let's take a closer look at two of them.

First is the compromise of non-public personal information (NPPI) or loss of data through the utilization of mobile devices. The consequences of an NPPI breach would be high, violating customer privacy provisions of the Gramm-Leach-Bliley Act and other regulations. Meanwhile, hackers are constantly attacking systems to access this information. The constant headlines of data breaches—everywhere from hotels to online streaming services—makes it a likely occurrence. As a result, the inherent risk is high.

Next, we look at what an institution can do to mitigate these risks. It can encrypt NPPI stored on portable devices. Let's estimate this control to be about 80 percent effective. Another preventative measure is antivirus and firewall software for portable devices that store or transmit NPPI. While some machines are set to automatically update these programs, others rely on customers to update it themselves—and busy customers often forget to do this. As a result, we'll estimate this control to be about 60 percent effective. Averaged together, the controls for preventing a breach of NPPI data through mobile devices are about 70 percent effective.

When working together, these tools are strong enough to largely mitigate the inherent risk of the activity, leaving low residual risk.

Now let's look at a risk an institution has less control over: unauthorized access to customer information due to a customer's lost or stolen mobile device. In 2014 in the U.S., an estimated 2.1 million smartphones were stolen,[80] while 3.1 million were lost. That's 5.2 million devices that were separated from their owners. The good news is that most stolen phones are in demand for their hardware, not their data, making the likelihood of a hack relatively low. However, the consequences for any breach of data are high, making authorized access an inherently high risk.

There are several controls to mitigate this risk, the majority of which are in the hands of the customer. First, the customer can report the lost or stolen device to the FI, enabling the institution to block access from the device. Second, lost or stolen devices can be locked with a passcode and remotely wiped clean of data.

Both of these methods are effective, but only if the customer notices their device is missing and then takes the appropriate steps. About 60 percent of wireless customers have a PIN or passcode on their smartphones or tablets, according to wireless trade association CTIA.[81] Also, not everyone has enabled the setting on their phone to remotely wipe them. That makes this control about 60 percent effective. Notifying the financial institution requires initiative on the part of the customer. Also, it may not cross the customer's mind to contact the institution. As a result, this control is only about 60 percent effective.

Averaged together, the controls for when a customer's device is lost or stolen are 60 percent effective. Given the relatively low likelihood that someone will use the device to hack into a financial institution's system and the moderate strength of the controls, it leaves the institution with moderate residual risk.

These are just two examples of the elements of risk that need to be assessed and mitigated when looking to expand the customer base for mobile and internet banking. When this approach is applied broadly across all the potential risks, the result is a thorough, enterprise-wide assessment of the true risks an activity poses and the ability of an institution is to manage them. These discussions raise important questions to help uncover and manage risks, providing insights into how an institution can best deploy its resources to the most critical areas.

By bonding strategic planning and risk management, an institution not only makes more educated decisions about the potential pitfalls and benefits of an activity, it also allows it to more effectively allocate capital to manage risk. When it's clear where the greatest residual risk lays, an institution can decide whether an activity is worth undertaking and where it needs to strengthen its controls.

DIGGING DEEPER: APPLYING RISK ASSESSMENT KNOWLEDGE

Now that we know how a risk assessment should work, let's look at a few real-world examples to understand how one institution might assess a few common risks and controls. We'll address Bank Secrecy Act, anti-money laundering, and Office of Foreign Assets and Control (BSA/AML/ OFAC), protecting sensitive customer data, compliance and cyber risks.

In conducting this exercise, we'll use the same scales as before.

Inherent Risk	Event Impact	Probability
Low (1)	Insignificant (1)	Remote (1)
Moderate-Low (2)	Minor (2)	Unlikely (2)
Moderate (3)	Moderate (3)	Possible (3)
High-Moderate (4)	Significant (4)	Likely (4)
High (5)	Catastrophic (5)	Certain (5)

Residual Risk	Control	Control Impact	% Effective
Low (1)	Low (1)	Very Important (5)	100%
Moderate-Low (2)	Moderate-Low (2)	Significant (4)	75-99%
Moderate (3)	Moderate (3)	Moderate (3)	50-75%
High-Moderate (4)	High-Moderate (4)	Minor (2)	21-49%
High (5)	High (5)	Unimportant (1)	1-20%

BSA/AML/OFAC

Bank Secrecy Act, anti-money laundering, and Office of Foreign Assets and Control (BSA/AML/OFAC) are critically important to any financial institution due to the significant reputational and regulatory risks associated with them. The FFIEC recommends financial institutions conduct a BSA/AML risk assessment every 12 to 18 months or when new products or services are introduced, existing products and services change, or higher-risk customers open or close an account.[82] The steps are the same as with every other kind of risk:

1. Identify BSA/AML/OFAC risks with relevant risk controls.
2. Assign impact and probability to each BSA/AML/OFAC risk to understand each risk's potential effect on the organization
3. Assign and prioritize controls for each BSA/AML/OFAC risk to manage risk mitigation
4. Define residual risk for BSA/AML/OFAC for a deeper dive into the total risk and a more consistent risk assessment

When assessing BSA/AML/OFAC, identify potential risk categories by looking at the institution's products, services, customers, transactions, and geographic locations as well as the regulations that must be followed. There's no shortage of areas to assess, including funds transfers, foreign correspondent accounts, and Customer Due Diligence (CDD).

In this case, let's look at the risk of failing to file suspicious activity reports (SARs).

Risk: Failing to file timely SARs.

Event Impact: Catastrophic. Failing to file suspicious activities reports and other BSA violations are a common source of enforcement actions. Falling short can have tremendous regulatory repercussions.

Probability: Possible. Just because you tell staff to do something, that doesn't mean they'll do it. Without a structure in place to ensure that reports are filed in a timely fashion, it's entirely possible something will fall through the cracks.

Inherent risk. Catastrophic. While the probability is only moderate, the potential consequences are so dire that the risk remains very high.

Fortunately, there are a variety of controls that can reduce the risk of a financial institution failing to properly file SARs.

- Policies and procedures
- Training
- Regular audits
- QC/QA processes

Let's look at policies and procedures.

Control: Policies and procedures

Impact: Significant. Well-drafted policies and procedures spell out the specific steps that should be taken and assign roles and responsibilities. They provide an important roadmap to ensure that every report is properly filed.

Effectiveness: 80%. There is always a chance that someone doesn't followthe policies and procedures. Assessments have shown occasional lapses.

Residual risk: Low. This strong control will go a long way towards reducing risk.

When combined with other controls, including training and regular audits, the residual risk can fall even further. It depends on the institution.

PROTECTING CUSTOMER DATA

Protecting customers' sensitive data is more than just a sacred duty. It's a regulatory requirement. A Gramm-Leach-Bliley Act risk assessment should identify reasonably foreseeable internal and external threats that could result in unauthorized disclosure, misuse, alteration, or destruction of information and assets.

Unauthorized access comes in many forms. In this case, let's consider the risk that an employee will successfully access or misuse data.

Risk: Employee unauthorized access or misuse of sensitive consumer information.

Event Impact: Catastrophic. It's a violation of federal law and could result in reputational damage to the institution.

Probability: Possible. With no controls it's easy enough to access data, but the average employee isn't likely to try to steal data.

Inherent Risk Rating: High-Moderate. While there is a lot of opportunity to steal data, the vast majority of employees aren't looking to commit a crime.

Now let's look at the controls the institution has in place to mitigate this risk. There are a variety of controls designed to limit unnecessary access to data. They include:

- Access restrictions based on job responsibilities
- Requiring individual identification and authentication for desktop log-on
- Formal policies that define password parameters and rules (no Post-its with passwords on monitors)
- Requirements for periodic review of access rights
- Termination protocols and checklists
- Secure disposal measures to properly dispose of consumer information when no longer needed
- Requirement for acknowledgement and acceptance of confidentiality/non-disclosure agreements before permitting access to confidential data or systems
- Employee privacy/GLBA training

Each of these controls should be individually reviewed and risk assessed. Then an aggregate residual risk score should be calculated. To better understand how this works, let's assess the first control by impact and probability.

Control: Access restrictions based on job responsibilities.

Impact: Important. The fewer people who have access to data, the safer the data is, and this control limits who has access. However, there will still be many people with access to the data, and logging into someone else's account to access data remains a possibility.

Effectiveness: 90% It's very hard to log in without access, assessments have shown.

Residual Risk: Low. With the controls in place, it's less likely that employees will be able to misuse sensitive data since fewer people will have it. Additional controls are necessary to reduce risk further.

COMPLIANCE

Ask any financial institution about its top challenges, and compliance is almost certain to make the list. From understanding new regulations to following existing rules to tracking exam and audit findings, managing compliance is an increasingly onerous and risky task.

Risk: Exam or audit findings fall through the cracks and aren't properly addressed in a timely fashion.

Event Impact: Catastrophic. Regulators will not be happy if identified problems aren't actively addressed. Failing to properly manage them can result in regulatory action.

Probability: Likely. With the increasing number of audits generating more and more findings, it's very possible that a finding could be lost in the shuffle.

As with most risks, there are a variety of controls that can reduce the risk exposure. They include:

- Policies and procedures
- Automated tracking system
- Board reporting

Let's assess an automated tracking system as a control.

Impact: Very important. An automated system ensures that every audit and exam finding is logged and tracked with someone assigned responsibility for follow through. It can provide reminders that actions are necessary and make it obvious which findings have been addressed and which are on their way.

Effectiveness: 90%. An automated system will very likely ensure that audit and exam findings are not forgotten. Human error remains a small factor, as sometimes people fail to properly use the system, but training can further increase the probability of proper usage.

Residual risk: Low. An automated tracking system greatly reduces the risk of failing to correct the errors that auditors and examiners identify.

CYBER RISK

Cybersecurity is a top concern for every financial institution. From reputational harm to regulator wrath, the cost of a breach is high.

Risk: Hackers aim a malicious attack at the institution's systems.

Event Impact: Catastrophic. The consequences of unauthorized access into the institution's systems are incredibly severe. Private customer data could be stolen or changed. Funds could be stolen. The institution could be locked out of its system. It could be a nightmare.

Probability: Certain. Cyber criminals are constantly looking for new victims and testing systems for vulnerabilities to exploit. It's a certainty that there are intruders trying to get into the network on a regular basis.

Inherent Risk Rating: Catastrophic. Not only is it likely that cyber criminals are trying to access the system, but if they did get in, it would cause tremendous damage.

Now let's look at the controls the institution has in place to mitigate these risks. After all, going offline isn't a viable option in the modern business world. There are a variety of network security protocols and controls designed to prevent and/or detect unauthorized access and cybersecurity incidents. They include:

- Anti-virus software on desktops and servers, with patches obtained from secure sites
- Anti-malware software installed on critical servers and on end-point devices, with signatures updated nightly
- Defense in Depth (DiD) program, including intrusion detection/ intrusion prevention systems.
- Semi-annual threat and vulnerability testing and attack and penetration tests
- Centralized monitoring via security incident and event management (SIEM)
- Perimeter firewall systems

Let's assess the first control by impact and effectiveness.

Control: Anti-virus software on desktops, servers, and host, with patches obtained from secure sites.

Impact: Significant. Anti-virus software should be quite effective in protecting systems, but there is always the possibility that there's an attack from a new virus that hasn't been discovered yet. Also, every machine must be patched for this to be effective. One machine could leave the whole network exposed.

Effectiveness: Possible. New viruses are being developed all the time and there are many malicious actors actively working to access systems, yet assessments have shown this control to regularly work.

Residual Risk: High-Moderate. Even though there are a great many controls to limit the possibility of a cyberattack, risk still remains, due to the evolving nature of cybersecurity threats.

This score is not an indictment of the IT department. IT should be appreciated for everything it does to protect the institution. Without its efforts, it's almost guaranteed that the institution would have been hacked by now. Instead, the risk assessment lets the board and management know that it needs to continue to invest heavily in cybersecurity. If the assessment indicated low cyber risk, the board and management might feel free to reallocate resources to another area of the institution —and in a world of rapidly advancing cyber threats, that's a mistake.

This exercise should be repeated for other areas of cyber risk, including the vendor management program. Take the time to not just identify potential risks, but also controls such as:

- A centralized vendor risk management program designed to address the adequacy of information security practices of third parties
- Due diligence prior to third-party engagement
- Enhanced due diligence for high-risk and critical vendors
- Defined data protection standards for third-party vendors with authorized access to data

Be realistic in how effective these controls will be in the real-world environment and how likely they are to work. Acknowledge that when it comes to cyber risk, there are few guarantees. Look at each control individually. It's not about being alarmist or giving friends a passing grade. It's about shaking off biases and looking at each control with a practical eye.

The takeaways from the sample assessments are clear. Inherent risk is often high. Some controls are more effective than others. Residual risk can often be lowered through a combination of controls.

Risk is a continuum. Therefore, there are no right or wrong risk or control scores. Scores are simply information, just like a customer's credit score. If an institution decides that an activity poses too much risk or that its controls are insufficient for managing those risks, then it can decide to discontinue the activity or consider new controls, just as it would decide whether or not to extend a loan based on a credit score. No institution wants its rating agency to adjust credit scores just to make a loan a slam dunk. It wants to know the truth so it can make an accurate credit decision.

The key to creating reliable risk assessments is consistency and awareness of potential biases. Management will be able to better utilize the information from risk assessments if the scoring processes are consistent. Every institution has different objectives, risk tolerances, and circumstances. Risk assessors should be encouraged to consider these unique attributes while also looking outside the institution to recognize risks and opportunities that are likely to impact similar organizations. Risk assessment must be an ongoing process, one where assessors are empowered with a broad base of knowledge and encouraged to think critically. When everyone is on the same page and aware of the same potential hang ups, risk assessments are far more likely to accurately represent risk and contribute to business success.

Cyber risk management isn't about being alarmist or giving friends a passing grade. It's about shaking off biases and looking at each control with a practical eye.

CHAPTER NINE

AUDITS & FINDINGS MANAGEMENT

Compliance officers have a great saying—if it isn't
documented, it didn't happen.

B y now, you should understand how to identify, assess, monitor, and
mitigate risk. While I can't emphasize enough the importance of the
risk assessment process and how it ties into strategic decision making,
there is more to ERM and the risk management lifecycle—three more
steps, to be exact. They are: evaluating the control environment, communicating findings, and remediation.

Risk Management Lifecycle

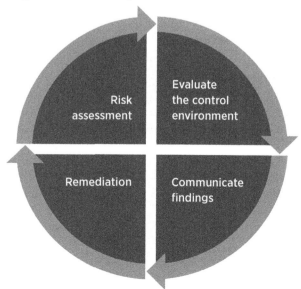

EVALUATING THE CONTROL ENVIRONMENT

Enterprise risk management is only as strong as the components it's built on. That makes review and testing of internal controls an essential element of ERM. It allows an institution to examine the effectiveness or veracity of a process, report, or other metrics.

In an ideal world, controls would be reviewed independently and objectively by someone who had no personal involvement in developing or executing the programs being reviewed, but that's not practical at many institutions. It's still possible to assess the effectiveness of a program and deliver findings and recommendations.

Reviewing the control environment requires these five key elements:

1. Support & Access

Auditors (or those conducting reviews) must be independent and able to objectively assess the operations of an institution. When they report to their boss or their FI's executives, they are sometimes afraid to report egregious violations or other types of findings that uncover questionable management. They don't want to rat out a coworker or lose their jobs for simply being the messenger.

That's why there should be policies protecting auditors from retaliation. It should also go without saying that auditors should not be fired because of reports, and any type of disciplinary action taken against them should be reviewed by the board.

In addition, auditors must be able to obtain work papers and test samples from business units. To facilitate their audits or reviews, auditors should have the authority to communicate with business units and employees without gatekeeping or red tape. While executives are protective of their resources, audits and reviews are like a health checkup. If you stop going to your primary doctor for check-ups, the results could be much worse.

Once audits and reviews are complete, financial institutions should report significant observations, findings, and recommendations directly to the board. While it's important to provide an opportunity to respond and clarify, that courtesy should never be interpreted as an invitation for business lines to obscure and modify an auditor's assessment.

2. Independence

The best reports are those that can objectively assess any business function. Unfortunately, human nature prevents most people from being able to objectively assess their own work. There is an actual scientific term for judging our own work more favorably than our peers would: illusory superiority. That's why most professions have instilled peer reviews and other types of practices to allow fresh, unbiased eyes to evaluate work.

The same idea endures when testing the control environment. People who help build a compliance program or craft the policies, procedures, and internal controls will not be as accurate judges of their work as someone who has not spent their time crafting it.

3. Risk-Based

FIs are required to comply with thousands of laws, regulations, and internal processes. However, resources are finite. Auditors must take the same approach as all the functional federal regulators—to allocate their resources to assess riskier practices or areas with a heightened risk for non-compliance or consumer harm. This means that the depth and frequency of an audit should consider the level of risk.

Auditors should not spend their time reinventing the wheel. A good practice is to review risk assessments, focusing on the areas where inherent risk is highest and audit the effectiveness of controls. If those controls are not mitigating the risk, this can have a dire impact on the institution.

A good control review plan should also take into account previous examinations and findings created by examiners. If an independent party has already identified an area of weakness, auditors should look at the activity undertaken to resolve deficiencies and ensure effectiveness. In addition, they can turn to recent enforcement actions and supervisory priorities to determine areas of perceived risk and regulatory scrutiny.

Don't forget about the complaints! Consumer complaints can unveil tricky areas of compliance risk such as UDAAP and fair lending.

4. Expertise & Training

Whether they are examining financial statements, regulatory compliance, or operational risk, auditors need to be knowledgeable about their field or they will not be effective. A common complaint I have heard from compliance officers is that they know more about compliance than the auditors and are often teaching them on the job. Auditors' teams will lose the respect, collaboration, and buy-in from those they audit if they are not knowledgeable.

Auditors need appropriate training and understanding of the processes they assess—otherwise, the results of the audit and the working relationships between the auditor and the institution will be lackluster. Auditors may not be the authority on a specific regulation, but they should have access to specialists or the tools to understand what they are auditing. That means they should be up to date with regulatory/institutional changes.

5. Technology

From organizing files to planning audits, technology makes auditors more effective. Depending on the level of complexity, risk profile, and size of the institution, audits can become unwieldy without the right tools. A technology partner that understands the types of reviews or audits required to be performed by an institution can be a valuable relationship. It should also support your institution's operations, foster collaboration, and make the job of organizing and retaining documents and presenting and resolving findings seamless. The right technology can make the entire process more efficient.

PRIORITIZING REVIEWS

Risk management is all about prioritizing. It identifies areas that require the most attention so that the necessary resources can be allocated. There are more functional areas and processes to review or audit at a financial institution than could ever be reviewed or audited, making it essential to prioritize areas that pose the greatest risk.

When prioritizing audits, focus on requirements first. Several audits are required by regulation, law, or contract such as the BSA, SAFE Act, and ACH compliance. A good audit program will ensure required audits are scheduled annually or as required.

Required audits are not the only ones that should be performed on an annual or periodic basis. Each institution is unique and will have its own sets of risks. Auditors should focus their attention on areas that pose a significant risk to the institution. This information can be found in risk assessments, supervisory guidance, prior examination/audit reports, and consumer complaints. They should also consider the areas that have not been reviewed or audited in a while and ensure those are given the proper weight while crafting the audit plan.

Compliance officers have a great saying—if it isn't documented, it didn't happen. But this is also true for auditors. Reviews and audits are meant to provide high levels of assurance. That means auditors should not solely rely on verbal attestations. Instead, they should scrupulously obtain samples and evidence to back up assessments and findings.

Risk professionals understand the importance of bringing in different perspectives—whether for determining the inherent risk of a product or conducting a control assessment. Auditors should also leverage different perspectives when it comes to getting the full picture.

When attempting to understand a department's processes, they should speak to more than just the department head. Department heads are great at knowing what policies or procedures state, but the frontline is in the best position to explain what they do on a day-to-day basis (which sometimes conflicts with a written document). Speaking to more than one individual can help uncover process deficiencies or outdated policies.

It's also helpful to consider what's new at the financial institution. Sometimes new products and services make it out the door before being properly vetted. Auditors should identify any new product, service, or process that may change the risk landscape at the institution and include it in the audit plan. Then, they should audit controls mitigating the risks of these new products and services to ensure they are effective or in need of remediation.

THE EVOLVING AUDIT

Audits aren't known for variability. While there might be a small change due to a regulatory change or hot button, FIs typically have a relatively consistent audit program from year to year. The predictable and formulaic audit programs that have served FIs well for most of banking's history are another victim of the COVID-19 pandemic.

The radical change in strategic planning and operations requires a nimble audit program. The board and management need to know whether changes such as borrower concessions, new loan programs, and changes to the strategic plan are performing as expected and whether they are creating undue risk.

This necessitates four key changes in audit programs:

1. **Proactive.** Audit programs need to be as proactive as possible to understand changes in the business model.
2. **More frequent.** Audit frequency needs to be adjusted to align with changes in the business model. Waiting for the next scheduled audit to determine the impact of major changes is risky.
3. **Depth & breadth.** The depth of testing may need to change based on the breadth of changes.
4. **New internal controls.** Institutions will need to test additional internal controls for effectiveness.

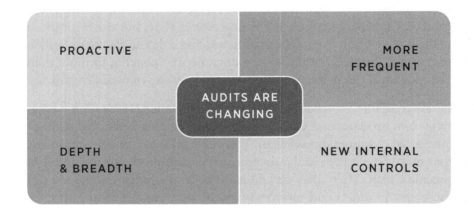

Gap analysis remains critical to the success of an audit program. Evaluating the effectiveness of each control/response uncovers these gaps.

COMMUNICATING TEST & AUDIT FINDINGS

Test & audit results tell a story. They show where an FI has succeeded and where it has struggled. It also shows opportunity. But like the proverbial tree falling in the forest, audit results mean nothing if they aren't shared—and shared in a way that makes them informative and usable.

When explaining test and audit results to the board, focus on key findings. The board isn't interested in a play-by-play. It doesn't care about the results of every test and audit. It doesn't need to know about an ineffective internal control if it's a minor control and the risk is mitigated by other controls or if it's a low-risk issue. The board wants the important takeaways—the type of information that will feed into strategic planning and decision making.

Presentations and reports should be simple and short. Think of an inverted pyramid. Include the most important information at the top, with a heavy emphasis on graphs, charts, and heat maps that can quickly convey key points. Anything that's nice to know, but not essential, should go at the bottom. Busy board members don't always make it to the end of a document so nothing important should be left for the last page.

If a major control mitigating a high risk is ineffective, the board will want to know about it. If there has been an increase in flood insurance errors, a very common source of enforcement actions, the board will want to know. These are issues that could result in serious harm to the institution.

After reviewing test and audit findings, the board will have the information it needs to determine where resources should be allocated and understand exactly how much risk the institution is exposed to.

RESOLVING FINDINGS

Findings. Exceptions. Deficiencies.

No matter what they are called, findings are the culmination of the audit and exam processes. They uncover risk, which exposes deficient policies, procedures, and other controls so that they can be promptly remediated.

Every institution has findings. A financial institution may have anywhere from 10 to 30 audits generating findings each year, not to mention exam results, ad hoc internal management reviews of products, services, and processes, and critical third-party vendor reviews, among others.

Identifying and promptly correcting findings is essential to minimizing risk and avoiding a potential enforcement action down the line, making careful findings management critical to success. From assigning responsibility for remediation to understanding the source of the problem to ongoing monitoring to ensure that the problem has been resolved, good findings management tracks findings from discovery to resolution and reports on the results. Poor findings management can have dire consequences.

Consider a study on the role of regulatory reporting during the financial crisis. It found that institutions with higher reporting quality were less likely to require additional regulatory intervention and much less likely to fail.[83]

It's not surprising to see that institutions with poor reporting struggle more with regulators, but it does raise a question. Is the poor reporting the result of the reporting process, or is poor findings management feeding incomplete or missing information into the report?

It's probably a little of both. Institutions with a good handle on findings management are in the best position to provide clear explanations and resolution reports to management. They know the source of the finding and what changed to ensure the problem doesn't recur.

Unfortunately, there are many ways to mismanage findings.

Is poor reporting the result of the reporting process, or is poor findings management feeding incomplete or missing information into the report?

Forgetting to follow up on a finding. It sounds like the most basic element of findings management, but that doesn't mean some institutions aren't getting it wrong. With so much going on, it's surprisingly easy to overlook a finding. A manager emails a staff member to follow up on an issue, and the well-meaning staffer plans to get to it, but then it slips through the cracks and no one takes responsibility for it. The staffer gets distracted by other tasks and the manager feels like that box has already been checked by emailing their colleague.

Oversights like this can have disastrous results. It's bad enough to have a repeat finding, but if that finding was time sensitive in the first place, it can end up costing the institution.

Imagine a mortgage lender that discovered that the floor rate on its adjustable-rate loans was listed incorrectly, which caused the institution to charge clients incorrectly. If the institution overcharged 1,000 borrowers $20 per month, that's $20,000 per month. If the institution self-discovered the problem while doing quality checks of its documents, it could promptly correct the discrepancy and minimize the amount of time it overcharged borrowers.

Now imagine that the institution had waited until its next audit or exam to follow up on the finding, and it turns out nothing had been done to correct the problem. The institution would have to repay borrowers $240,000 a year or $480,000 over two years. That money would have to come from capital, and with today's tight margins, it could be very financially damaging. It also doesn't account for any enforcement actions or potential civil money penalties to be paid, especially if it becomes a repeat finding.

Institutions can avoid these kinds of risks with a findings management process that ensures issues are identified, tracked, and promptly remediated.

Not recognizing the importance of a finding. With so many findings, it's tempting to take a quick look at a finding before deciding what to do about it. In the triaging process, it can be easy to misunderstand the true impact of the finding.

I know of an institution that discovered a weakness in its vendor management process. While the institution was collecting documents from each critical vendor as part of its due diligence process, it wasn't reviewing these reports to assess how strong the vendor's financials were. This may seem like a minor issue, but it can have far-reaching consequences.

In the case of this institution, not reviewing the financials turned out to be a significant problem because the vendor was having financial problems. A timely review of the documents would have uncovered red flags about the vendor and its financials, which were getting worse. To try and right the ship, the vendor had made changes to how it was offering its products and services, which had increased the risk of a potential data breach, but the institution had no idea.

Presented with an opportunity to correct this oversight, the institution should have used its findings management program to log and track the SSAE 18 finding. Instead, the finding got put on the back burner. As a result, the institution renewed its contract with the vendor when it would have benefitted from renegotiating the contract to include provisions to better protect its data or finding a new vendor altogether.

Treating every finding as equally important. Some institutions follow the exact same timeline for every finding. For example, it might require that every finding be acknowledged within 30 days.

While on the surface this seems like a best practice, in truth not every finding presents the same risk. With limited resources, an institution needs to prioritize findings and resolve the most critical ones with urgency. Rather than have standard timeline for completion, the process should instead require that every finding be risk assessed within a fixed number of days. That will give the institution the information it needs to ensure the most important findings are addressed first.

Not following up on changes to internal controls. It's not enough to adjust or introduce new internal controls to resolve a finding and move on. It's necessary to revisit these controls to ensure they are performing as intended.

For example, a finding might show that employees haven't been following funds availability policies. Frontline staff trained to do everything they can to help customers might think that waiving funds availability rules for a good customer is an example of "going the extra mile" and providing exemplary customer service. Staff doesn't realize the policy protects both the institution and the customer from losing money on a bad check.

To address this finding, the institution might decide to retrain staff on the policy. While this can be an effective approach, the institution won't know for sure until it goes back and reviews whether staff has done a better job consistently complying with the policy after training. Ongoing monitoring may show a significant improvement in compliance, but it also might demonstrate just a slight improvement.

Findings are a form of measurement. They show an institution where it needs improvement. A risk can't be managed if no one is aware of the problem.

For each finding, institutions should ask:

- What internal controls failed?
- Have changes to internal controls reduced risk?
- Are additional controls needed?

While no institution *wants* findings, they are a valuable tool for managing risk and ensuring institution policies and procedures are followed.

Handled correctly, findings provide institutions with the opportunity to improve operations and reduce risk while demonstrating to examiners that the institution is proactively working to ensure safety and soundness.

It's essential that findings generated from audits and exams are managed promptly and efficiently. Automating the complex findings process helps financial institutions conserve resources, improve findings data visibility, and audit document controls. When issues are known and addressed, organizations are both ready for future audits and protected from potential shortcomings within their own systems.

The better an institution manages its findings, the less likely it is to have them in the future. There needs to be a clear and detailed process for findings response and remediation, including a centralized place for data, findings prioritization, task assignment and timelines, and follow-up.

In an ideal world, every institution's enterprise risk management program would be perfect and without weakness. But the truth is that every institution has some areas of risk that need work. Changing conditions guarantee it. That's why it's important to have a system for organizing findings. On its own, one finding can be simple to track. A handful is manageable. But the more findings an institution has to juggle, and the more complex those findings are, the harder it is to keep everything straight.

Every institution needs a systematic, centralized system for tracking, remediating, and documenting findings to ensure nothing gets lost in the shuffle. Best practices suggest:

- While findings vary in their size and importance, each finding must be handled consistently. Exceptions make for sloppy record keeping and increase the likelihood of it getting lost or forgotten.

- Documents, policies, and procedures should be stored in one place whenever possible. Staff shouldn't maintain piecemeal files across the institution. That includes logs of all remediation activities.

- If an action isn't documented, then in the eyes of regulators it didn't happen. Document meetings, risk identifications, assessments, and remediation.

- For every finding, make it clear who is responsible for overseeing the remediation plan. Document which tasks are assigned to which employees and carefully track each employee's progress.

- Keep a traceable audit trail or log of all activities, noting what was changed, when, and by whom.

- Risk management teams face constant distractions as new risks emerge and existing risks evolve. Don't let old findings get lost in the shuffle. Have a method in place to ensure the institution actively follows up on all known findings on a regular basis.

- When it comes to exam prep, institutions should be able to easily discuss all their findings and how close the institution is to remediating them.

Once audits are completed and reported on and findings are thoroughly remediated, the risk management lifecycle begins again. Or, more precisely, it continues uninterrupted. With risk management, there is no beginning and there is no end. It's an ongoing process, with different areas and business lines in different phases (and sometimes even multiple phases) at the same time. There's no rest for risk managers and auditors.

CHAPTER TEN

SETTING STRATEGY

Simply put, when we as a business make strategic decisions with risk in mind, the outcome is increased value for all shareholders and stakeholders.

T he link between risk and strategy has evolved significantly over the past decade or so. For example, when COSO debuted its original risk management framework in 2004, it looked a lot like a Rubik's Cube, that impossible 3-D puzzle you remember from childhood. The framework and its cube had a narrow focus on identifying risk and avoiding potentially negative consequences. Strategy barely got a mention.

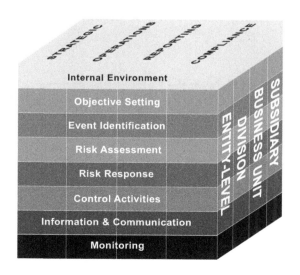

Under the old framework, which was an innovative concept at the time, a risk assessment was like a map that identified potholes but didn't label roads or destinations. The tool had some practical use, but it couldn't help you figure out where you were going. It told you where not to go. It did nothing to stop you from wandering aimlessly, wasting time and resources. Despite the cube's three-dimensional appearance, in retrospect this model was fairly one dimensional. While it effectively assessed and communicated risk, the exclusion of a link between risk and strategy meant that resources weren't always allocated efficiently when it came to the control environment. As resources are always scarce, this was just bad business, and it led to situations where overallocations on controls were potentially counterproductive to the organization's goal achievement. This is why the link between risk and strategy is so important. Consequently, COSO added and, moreover, emphasized this link in subsequent guidance.

An understanding of the evolution of enterprise risk management is key, as this is still a discipline well in its infancy. Today we understand that risk assessments are more than just tools for avoiding risk. They can help identify opportunities to exploit, uncover performance shortfalls more quickly, connect business lines and functions, and promote information sharing across an institution to create a more comprehensive picture of threats and opportunities. Paired with strategy, risk management can help create a roadmap to successfully guide an institution from Point A to Point B, and swiftly correct course as necessary.

STRATEGY

Remember the illustration of the COSO ERM framework back in Chapter 3 that resembled a DNA double helix? In our earlier discussion, we cited the components and principles of an effective ERM program. As a reminder, they fit into five categories:

- Governance & Culture
- Strategy & Objective-Setting
- Performance
- Review & Revision
- Information, Communication & Reporting

Each of these five components supports the business model at every stage: mission, vision, and core values; strategy development; business objective formulation; implementation and performance; and enhanced value.

This approach to risk management reminds us that successful institutions weave risk management and strategy seamlessly into their DNA.

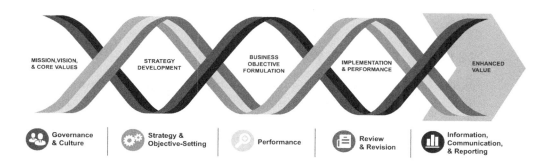

They leverage the work of their risk assessments to maximize their value. This has three key strategic advantages:[84]

1. It helps an institution recognize when strategy or strategic objectives don't align with mission, vision, and values.
2. When developing and evaluating strategies, it considers the impact of risk.
3. It highlights the potential for risk to interfere with strategy execution and performance.

The output of these strategic advantages collectively is enhanced value. Simply put, when we as a business make strategic decisions with risk in mind, the outcome is increased value for all shareholders and stakeholders. This increased value is often tangible and measurable, such as an increase in profits, an increase in stock price, or the payment of dividends. Whether a business is publicly traded or not, this value add is core to the existence and continued competitiveness of the firm.

It also introduces one very important question: how does an institution set strategy?

SETTING STRATEGY

Earlier we defined strategy as a high-level plan designed to achieve one or more goals. It requires setting individual goals and determining the actions necessary to achieve each of those goals, all while ensuring those actions and goals will help an institution act upon its mission (why it exists), vision (goals for the future), and core values (beliefs and ideals) in a way that ultimately adds value.

Setting strategy is the job of the board, but many boards err by mistaking strategy for a goal. They might say their strategy is to grow deposits, penetrate deeper into the marketplace, or spend more on cybersecurity, but those aren't strategies. They are goals. They are missing a critical element of strategy: the how.

Let's consider the mission, vision, and values of a hypothetical institution: First Mandalorian Bank.

Mission: We will provide exemplary personalized financial services in our market, delivering value to shareholders, customers, employees, and the local community.

Vision: Our dependable, customer-centric institution will be the area's leading small business lender, known for helping consumers, business owners, and the local community achieve financial success while rewarding employees and shareholders.

Values: Commitment, dependability, and efficiency.

It's not enough for First Mandalorian to say that its strategy is to be profitable or more profitable than last year. That is not a strategy. It's not specific, and it doesn't provide direction. It isn't measurable on a granular level, so it is difficult to monitor for success or failure. It also doesn't align with the mission, vision, or values of the institution. While every bank aims to make money, this bank's mission, vision, and values don't prioritize huge profits over the business of banking and serving the community.

Digging a little deeper, First Mandalorian's board might say its strategy is to increase margins, lower its cost of funds, make more profitable investments, or improve its efficiency ratio. These are all ways to increase profitability, but they aren't strategy. They are vague objectives lacking in specificity and measurability. Once again, they don't tie into mission, vision, and values. We don't know how increasing margins will contribute to meeting the bank's overall strategy or how the bank will know when it has achieved its objective.

Another common mistake is deciding to undertake a major project and calling it strategy without considering how that project would further the institution's mission, vision, or values. First Mandalorian could decide its strategy for next year is changing its core processor. Everyone knows switching cores is a major endeavor that takes at least a year (if you're lucky), but that doesn't automatically make it strategy. It's only strategy when it ties into the big picture. Until then, it's just an expensive project.

Let's take a look at how a core upgrade could be integrated into strategy. First Mandalorian could decide its strategy is to attract and retain small business customers by providing best-in-class treasury and payments services. This strategy could support the bank's small business lending vision, allowing it to attract and deliver greater value to small business customers and ultimately shareholders.

When assessing the risks associated with this strategy, First Mandalorian realizes that its current core processor can't efficiently support the best-in-class services it wants to offer. Integrating the services would require a patchwork of software systems that would be difficult to implement and not entirely reliable. Meanwhile the bank's current in-house core processor is increasingly resource dependent as the bank continually adds defenses to guard against cyber risk and the bank has been eyeing replacements for the past 18 months. On the other hand, implementing a new core is a massive undertaking that will require substantial costs and man hours.

Weighing increasing cyber risk and efficiency challenges against the heavy lift that is introducing a new core system, First Mandalorian finds that the short-term expenditure on a new core is worth the potential long-term benefits. It will make the bank a more dependable, valuable small business partner, consistent with this aspect of their overall strategic planning. Thus, the bank decides that a new core processor is the best way to move the strategy forward, making it a strategic objective. In this scenario, a new core processor is instrumental in implementing their strategy of increasing their small business client base. It also aligns with the bank's values by increasing efficiency.

There are plenty of other strategies First Mandalorian could consider. If it needed to grow deposits to meet demand for small business loans, its strategy might be to grow deposits through acquisition or entering a new market to increase funding for small business lending. If it's looking to increase efficiency and focus its attention on geographic areas where the bulk of their small business customers bank, it may want to reduce the branch network in areas with limited demand or where multiple offices overlap. Perhaps First Mandalorian wants to increase profitability by expanding its small business lending program by entering a niche market or diversifying its commercial lending with participation loans. If First Mandalorian specialized in serving the medical field, its strategy could include financing elective surgeries to bolster demand for its clients' medical services.

CONSIDERING THE IMPACT OF DIFFERENTIATION

As the board or senior leadership considers strategic directions, the group may be attracted to generic strategies. A generic strategy means a strategic direction that is utilized by many other similarly situated companies in different markets. This type of strategy appeals to leaders who want to take a safe path, and this notion of safety is rooted in the popularity of the generic strategy.

However, there are fundamental risks to pursing a generic strategy, which include failing to have competitive differentiation, failing to adapt to changing technology, and failure to sustain the strategic direction. A specific strategy that fundamentally provides for competitive differentiation has proven to be a tremendous advantage for organizations that make the correct choice.

The second major challenge to generic strategies is failing to adopt to changing technology. There are numerous banks that built out extensive branch networks to grow their borrowing base from 2010 to 2020, despite the growing number of customers that primarily interacted with their bank from their phone. This change in technology and consumer behavior represents a material threat to the generic growth strategy of building more branches.

The third major challenge is the failure to sustain the strategic direction with the generic strategy. Organizations will find it more challenging to inspire the team, justify changes in spending, and make personnel changes for a strategy that is generic or uninspiring. It will take a great leader and tremendous commitment to effectively implement a generic strategy, and many times people implement this type of approach while continuing to search for a better path.

CONSIDERING THE IMPACT OF RISK

All strategies come with some form of risk, and not all those risks are immediately obvious at the strategy development phase. Who would have guessed that elective surgeries would come to a halt when the COVID-19 pandemic made personal protective equipment (PPE) scarce and made doctors and patients wary of exposing themselves to the virus if it wasn't absolutely essential? While a risk assessment might not predict a pandemic, it should consider the likelihood and impact of reasonably foreseeable events such as a decreased demand for elective surgery.

When developing and evaluating strategy, risk-based data is essential. It goes back to the formula for inherent risk. Inherent risk is determined by the potential impact of an event by its very nature and the probability of it occurring naturally without regard to controls. In other words, strategy needs to consider the impact of risk and the potential of that risk to interfere with strategy execution and performance.

Let's go back to the example of First Mandalorian's strategy to attract and retain small business customers by providing best-in-class treasury and payments services, which involves changing core processors. A risk assessment is necessary to fully understand both the risks and the benefits of the strategy. Some of the questions the bank might ask include:

- Does the investment in new treasury and payments services (and by extension a new core) justify the potential returns?
- How does the bank expect to benefit from the initiative? (Examples: more competitive pricing, more functionality, the ability to offer new and innovative products and services, etc.)
- Does First Mandalorian have the internal resources to dedicate to such a huge project?
- Will it endanger the success of other strategic goals?
- Is this a product/service that First Mandalorian's small business customer base wants?
- What impact will the new core have on existing products and services? Will they have to be upgraded as well?
- What is the risk that the core change will significantly disrupt customers or staff workflows?
- How time sensitive is this project and how would delays impact the institution (customers, financials, etc.)?

Rather than just focus on the perceived benefits of the strategy, a risk assessment will uncover potential pitfalls, confirm strategic opportunities, and even identify other benefits or risks that hadn't been previously considered. This process allows an institution to understand the inherent risk of the strategy, consider controls that could help mitigate risk, and determine whether the strategy ultimately aligns with the institution's risk tolerance.

BREAKING DOWN STRATEGY INTO MEASURABLE GOALS & OBJECTIVES

Every strategy needs to be broken down into a plan with measurable milestones, objectives, and sub-objectives. This allows an institution to understand all the components that feed into the strategy, including dependencies. It shows what combination of activities will best help the institution achieve its goal.

These objectives are more than just a roadmap to the destination. They also help the board and management assess the risks of the overall strategy and ensure that the risk is consistent with the institution's risk appetite.

Going back to the core processor example, we know that changing the core will take a year, if not longer. It involves engaging multiple vendors, gathering pricing, negotiating a contract, prep work, assigning implementation to staff, training staff, potentially replacing existing products and services, launch week, marketing new products and services, teaching customers how to log in or use new systems, and many other steps.

Breaking down a strategy into objectives and sub-objectives makes it possible to more fully evaluate risk. Risks can be evaluated, and controls can be applied to every subcomponent, as necessary. It may seem like an overly granular approach to strategy, but it's the type of process that can improve the likelihood of success or help the board reach the decision that a strategy just isn't workable.

In some cases, a project management approach to evaluating strategic objectives may be necessary, especially when objectives must be met sequentially. This helps an institution understand the impact one objective can have on the completion of subsequent objections—and the project as a whole.

Let's take a few moments to understand why. There are some sub-objectives that, simply put, are essential to a strategy's success. If the institution fails to meet that sub-objective, it won't make its objective and ultimately the strategy will fail. For example, if staff isn't trained on how to use the new core and solutions, they won't be able to cross-sell new products and services or support customers with questions. That would ultimately cause the project to fail. Linking risks and controls with sub-objectives shows potential threats and weaknesses in the strategy and creates an opportunity to develop more or better controls or abort a strategy that's unlikely to succeed.

For this to happen, strategic objectives also need to be specific and quantifiable so that success can be measured. They should also be attainable. It's not enough for strategy to provide a broad idea of how profitability will be reached, such as increasing margins, lowering the cost of funds, making specific investments, or improving the efficiency ratio. Solid strategy execution involves breaking down objectives to a granular level that dictates specifically how a strategic objective will be met. For example, it may detail a specific combination of actions that will drive the project, from hiring new staff members to opening new demand deposit accounts.

Examples may include:

- Increase revenue 5 percent over the next 12 months
- Bring an online loan origination platform to market with specific features that will return 5 percent ROI within one year
- Decrease expenses by 10 percent
- Grow organically by 7 percent
- Decrease customer churn by 20 percent
- Develop a new business line that increases customer product adoption from 1.3 products to 2 products
- Reduce loan processing time by 1 day
- Respond to all customer emails within 2 hours
- Open a new branch in a market that adds $25 million in new assets by year-end
- Open 100 new accounts per month for the next 12 months
- Hire two new loan officers

These metrics should not be chosen at random. Just because something is measurable, doesn't mean it's valuable. There should be documented reasons why these objectives and sub-objectives support the proposed strategy, both on their own and collectively. For example, a strategy to increase brand awareness in the marketplace may include the objective to gain 25 new Facebook followers per month. Where did this number come from? Was it researched or chosen at random? How will this goal show increased brand awareness? How does it tie into other objectives to achieve sufficient brand awareness?

Risk informs strategy, but strategy also informs risk management. Specific and measurable goals will allow for key risk indicators (KRIs) and key performance indicators (KPIs) to be applied that will help your institution track its progress towards its overall strategic goals, understand its successes and struggles, and promptly correct course, if needed.

KRIs and KPIs must be monitored. To start, evaluate each KRI or KPI to understand its importance and value as an indicator. Then decide how often it will be monitored, who will monitor it, and thresholds that require reporting.

When deciding on reporting thresholds, remember that KRIs and KPIs are early warning systems. They give your institution the opportunity to adjust strategy and how it's achieved. For example, imagine your institution doesn't want its cost of funds to go above 0.5 percent. If you only report that figure during board meetings and the cost of funds has inched up to 0.6 percent, I can promise you it's not going to be a pleasant meeting. You'll have a flustered board and a fire drill on your hands. Imagine instead that you set up your reporting so that the board would get notification if the cost of funds hit 0.4 percent. That would give everyone time to correct course and avoid exceeding the institution's threshold. Being proactive with risk measurement and reporting can prevent negative outcomes.

Therefore, the most significant controls will be the ones that require the most frequent monitoring and reporting. An institution's internal testers including compliance and internal audit staff can play a role in testing these internal controls, freeing up risk managers to focus on mitigating risk.

The most important aspect of this process is accountability. Reports need to be delivered to someone who has the power to effect the appropriate level of change if something isn't performing as it should. Data has no value if it's not given to someone with the ability to move the needle.

It's also important to set dates and milestones to push projects forward. Once you've set a strategic goal, broken down its components, and risk assessed them, implementation dates need to be set. This accountability will help propel the project forward.

Data has no value if it's not given to someone with the ability to move the needle.

STRATEGY & BENCHMARKING

Setting strategy isn't just about looking inward. It also requires looking outward at peers and your local market.

Every financial institution should benchmark itself against its peers. From rate shopping to the FDIC's peer reports to mystery shopping and competitive intelligence, a smart way to begin strategizing is to look next door. The goal isn't to copy their ideas. It's to gain insights into your institution's competitive advantages and identify niches that aren't being served so that your institution can fill those needs better than your competitors.

For example, an institution may conduct benchmarking and a community needs assessment and realize that there are many living paycheck to paycheck who rely on payday loans when they encounter a financial emergency like a car wreck. Institutions can charge decent interest rates for these short-term, unsecured loans, which makes them an attractive addition to revenue increasing strategic goals.

The next step is to assess the risks of offering short-term, unsecured loans. Think about what success looks like and consider all the possible things that could go wrong to keep the institution from reaching that point. While highly profitable, these loans have higher default rates. The institution needs to determine what default rate it can accept and still make a profit on the entire portfolio of these loans. It must consider how many loans must be underwritten to return a profit and what size these loans can be. There are additional cost-related questions, such as internally building the appropriate infrastructure or engaging and then managing a vendor to provide the product. There are also compliance risk concerns, such as entering a market that's subject to increasing regulatory scrutiny. Benchmarking may also provide valuable insight here, as the FI's decision-making process may benefit from the knowledge of specific areas in which competitors have succeeded or failed regarding this product offering.

SETTING A FINTECH STRATEGY

Fintech is one of the buzziest trends in financial services, and no financial institution wants to be left behind. But with seemingly boundless opportunities, how do you know which fintech partnerships make sense for your FI?

Follow the strategy and risk management process.

Start with a clearly defined business strategy. Strategy, not technology, should drive your fintech decisions. Before considering any fintech partnerships, *make sure you have a clearly defined and communicated business strategy that aligns with your FI's objectives.*

Sometimes opportunities fall into our laps and seem serendipitous. Take a keen eye to these opportunities—don't jump right away. Instead, proactively seek out partnerships that will support your goals. Avoid signing on for a fintech partnership simply because it sounds cool or blindly adopting a promising new technology and then building a strategy around it. Only experiment with fintech if you have a goal and purpose in mind, and if engaging fintech firms is within your institution's established risk tolerance. Use your limited resources to explore fintech that can make a significant contribution to your institution. Experimenting with fintech partnerships that do nothing to drive bottom-line results may not be a good use of time and effort. It's all about what your institution wants to accomplish strategically and if that partnership can help you get there.

Often, a financial institution will direct IT staff to develop fintech partnerships. While IT has a lot of insight to offer, they don't have all the information to drive the decision. The board needs to communicate the financial institution's strategy and strategic goals. Then IT and other business lines can work together to understand the objectives and sub-objectives of the initiative and the potential risks they pose. For instance, an institution doesn't want to be caught off guard when an existing vendor stores data in a way that will not allow it to communicate with other technologies.

Scalability is a significant concern when assessing the long-term viability of a fintech partner. Having a strategy for fintech adoption can help an institution know what to look for when signing longer term vendor agreements, so it can determine if the vendor can grow with the institution's strategic goals in the not-too-distant future. Too often financial institutions focus on today's needs without putting in the time to consider what it hopes to accomplish three to five years from now. Other times, an institution changes its strategic direction and then is surprised to find out that its vendor can't support its new goals. Don't begin discussions with new fintech vendors that will be core to your institution's strategy until your institution has had serious conversations about its strategic direction. You can't comprehensively evaluate a new partner if you don't know what you'll need from them, both now and in the reasonably foreseeable future.

Only deploy fintech partnerships that make strategic sense. It shouldn't be a strictly business or tech initiative, but it should be an enterprise-wide strategic initiative.

THE BOARD AND STRATEGY

An engaged board is essential for successfully setting strategy, but not every board understands the depths of its responsibility. Some dust off their strategic plan every other year, patting themselves on the back for creating a beautiful slide deck with no substance. These boards are likely to have broad goals lacking in "the why" we discussed earlier. Nebulous concepts such as growing deposits, penetrating deeper into the marketplace, or spending more on cybersecurity fall well short of strategic development, as they aren't measurable and can't be linked with associated risks and monitored for performance.

Training is important to help boards understand why the institution requires specific, quantifiable strategic objectives as a part of the strategy development process and how linking risk data to these objectives will help them adapt the strategy and make better decisions.

It's also important to be strategic with which risk data is highlighted in board documents. Directors spend, on average, 70 percent of their time reviewing documents (quarterly reports, audit reviews, budgets, compliance) instead of developing strategy.[85]

That time can be reduced by delivering metrics in short, visual reports with elements like graphs, charts, and heat maps that tell them:

- What's going right?
- What's going wrong?
- What do you want the board to do?

The most important information should be on the first page, making it easy to pick out and understand key points. Let's say the board's goal is to grow revenue by 8 percent. One of the many objectives in reaching the goal is to open a certain number of deposit accounts. If the institution is behind in this goal, endangering the overall revenue growth goal, that information should be front and center. It's important information the board will want to know, and there's a good chance the board isn't going to read to the end of the report.

Board reports and presentation materials should be shared several days before a meeting so that the board has a chance to review and prepare. This makes for more productive board meetings and fosters conversations regarding risk and strategy that will ultimately benefit the institution.

The goal of risk reporting is to help the board become better decision makers, which is ultimately how value is added to shareholders and stakeholders. Risk assumptions will change. Strategy must change with it, or there is a risk that strategy will no longer align with the institution's risk tolerance and appetite.

CHAPTER ELEVEN

ALIGNING STRATEGY & ERM

When an institution has its eyes open to risk, it can see both the upside and the downside of risk.

I nertia is one of the greatest forces in the universe. Sir Isaac Newton dedicated the first law of motion to it: a body at rest will stay at rest unless an outside force acts on it.

He was talking about physics, but he may as well have been speaking about human nature. People generally maintain the status quo. We take the same route to work, order a drink at the same coffee shop, and read the same news sites every day.

We do this because it's easy and comfortable. We stick with what we know and regularly do because we perceive it as risky to make another choice. We don't often think about the cost of that choice because we've already made it.

But there are risks, and those risks have costs.

When we take the same route to work automatically, we're not considering that there might be a quicker, more efficient way to get there on that particular day. When we order from the same coffee shop, we're not thinking about the possibility that there might be another coffee shop we'd enjoy even more. When we read the same news sites, we're limiting the ideas that we're exposed to.

Most of the time, this isn't a big deal. But when you're running a business, inertia can create risk. This is particularly applicable to risk management. Back in the day, it was much simpler to run a financial institution. There was interest rate risk and credit risk and concerns about the physical security of the building. Risk management was a relatively small task.

Today thanks to the internet, the cloud, a huge influx of new regulations, and myriad other things, there's far more risk in running a financial institution. Yet many banks and credit unions continue to handle risk management the same way they did in simpler times. They use an ad hoc approach, dealing with issues as they come up, instead of having a unified process in place to identify, manage, and mitigate risks at an enterprise level.

They think it's working because they haven't encountered any major issues yet, but that's just because they don't know what they don't know. They don't know that:

1. **They're taking on much more risk than they think.** If you're not measuring risk, you're underestimating it. Can you imagine operating a business with no management team? Everyone would independently do what they thought was best and set their own priorities. Some people would care about doing a good job. Others wouldn't. It's a recipe for disaster. The same thing happens when there isn't a top-down approach to risk management. With no one in charge, there's no way to know what's important and what's getting done.

   Many institutions have faced hefty fines for violations of Bank Secrecy Act and Office of Foreign Assets Control regulations. The vast majority of those institutions didn't make a conscious decision to ignore federal rules and regulations, but they also didn't make a conscious decision to take the time to understand the magnitude of the risk and develop a good risk management program either. If they took the time to understand the potential fines and regulatory consequences of falling short, they'd have paid more attention to the issue.

2. **They are missing out on the opportunity to strategically engage in risk.** The best institutions are proactive, not reactive. ERM

makes it easier to objectively identify and assess both threats and opportunities, allowing the institution to make quicker, more informed decisions. Being the first to see an opportunity is a huge competitive advantage. Another advantage: uncovering a threat and responding appropriately before it causes damage.

Risk isn't a bad word. It's an opportunity, one where the potential cost should be carefully weighed. When an institution has its eyes open to risk, it can see both the upside and the downside of risk. On the upside, an FI can take advantage of business opportunities and carve out a competitive edge. It also lets the institution predict possible challenges, enabling it to potentially minimize disruptions. While there are always surprises, strategic risk management should lessen them, ensuring the institution is better prepared to deal with changing conditions.

New activities and business lines are more than just potential profit centers. They are also potential sources of risk that need to be carefully identified, measured, monitored, reported, and controlled. They need to align with a FI's overall strategy and business plan and give consumers fair access and treatment when it comes to financial services. A strong risk management system provides insights into new endeavors and prevents expensive missteps. Failing to manage risk impedes an institution's ability to achieve strategic goals, limiting its income and financial success.

3. **They aren't properly aligning management incentives and interests with strategic goals.** When an institution sets a strategic goal without weighing risks, it can encourage unethical, unsafe, and unsound business practices. A goal may be simple: open more credit card accounts. But if an institution fails to consider the risk of incentivizing staff to open accounts and the potential for internal fraud without strong policies, procedures, and other controls to create accountability, the result can be a scandal à la Wells Fargo.

It's not enough for an institution to achieve a strategic goal. It must do so in a way that supports the long-term health and success of the institution. That requires a thorough understanding of all the risks of that activity, including incentives, to ensure management is not sacrificing the institution's future for short-term gains. Brokers at WaMu were financially motivated to sell poorly documented subprime mortgages while management profited from those sales, turning a blind eye to risk. Their incentive-driven zeal drove WaMu into the ground.

4. **They're spending money in the wrong places.** When you don't have a system in place to objectively evaluate the amount of risk an activity presents, you're not using your resources wisely. Not all risks are equal. Some are very big while others are quite small. The risks posed by the potential loss of private customer data due to an insecure server are much greater than the risk of running out of business cards or the lawn growing too high.

5. **They miss the opportunity to detect risk in its infancy.** Risk may begin in one department or business line, but it rarely stays there. Institutions with well-developed enterprise risk management programs benefit from sharing information about risk that has been detected in one area of the organization before that risk can begin impacting other areas.

6. **They aren't operating as efficiently as they could be.** Decentralized risk management creates redundancies, inefficiencies, and discrepancies that waste time and money. Risk management overlaps areas including compliance, IT, vendor management, business continuity planning, operations, marketing, deposits, and lending. If there isn't a strong risk management system, it's likely these areas are duplicating each other's work and possibly coming to different conclusions. A strong risk management program eliminates silos so departments can build on and leverage each other's work, which results in better oversight, greater efficiency, and lower costs. It also makes it easier to understand what needs to be done and who is best best equipped to do it.

7. **They are endangering their long-term resiliency.** Want to know the difference between community banks that "thrived" during the Great Recession and the ones that just survived? The Federal Reserve Bank of Saint Louis found that thriving community banks with high CAMELS ratings "practiced forward-looking risk management with an eye toward long-term bank performance."[86] Institutions that neglect ERM are missing an opportunity to build a more resilient business.

When an institution doesn't have a clear way to measure risk, it often resorts to playing risk management Whack-A-Mole, using the same sized hammer to hit each mole. It's a wildly inefficient process. When an institution uses the same approach to tame each risk, it's overdoing it on the small risks and underestimating the effort needed to address the larger ones. It's much smarter to allocate resources to the biggest risks, but you can only do that if you understand and rank risks. I'm sure each one of those CEOs and management teams facing BSA and OFAC fines thought they were spending money in the right place.

Most people think of taking action as the riskier choice, however, inertia is just as risky. Instead of asking what would happen if it changed its risk management procedures, institutions should ask what would happen if they *didn't* change them.

Phrased another way, institutions should compare risk management models objectively and ask, "If we were choosing a risk management model today, which would be a better choice: an ad hoc model that addresses risks as they emerge or a top-down approach that measures, monitors, and mitigates risk across the entire enterprise?"

Looking at it that way, the risk of inertia is obvious.

Strategic success relies on thoughtful risk management across an institution. Enterprise risk management is more than fending off risks as they emerge. It's implementing controls, including policies and procedures, to ensure proper risk management both at the highest levels of strategic planning and in daily operations. It touches every department, looking at risk as a series of "what ifs" to determine how an institution can prevent that "what if" from becoming an eventuality.

How do seasoned risk professionals fight risk management inertia? They find ways to dismantle silos and develop processes to spark discussion about risk throughout the enterprise.

It's easier said than done, but with determination and a clear game plan, it's possible. We reached out to professional risk managers for their best silo-busting tips. Here's what they told us:

1. Give everyone a seat at the risk table.
When using a committee approach to risk management, think broadly

about which areas of the institution should be represented. IT and compliance may be top of mind, but areas like human resources, marketing, and deposit operations belong there too.

Risks intersect, and sometimes that intersection isn't apparent until the right person at the table brings up a new perspective. People rarely think outside their own lane, so it's important to bring all the drivers together. Once an initial discussion takes place, if a business line really has no tie to the initiative, it can be left out of future meetings. If extra support is needed, it can be called in.

When the door to discussion is wide open, it makes it much harder for something to sneak in undetected.

2. Integrate risk into processes.

Baking risk management into the beginning of any initiative ensures that every business line and department is aware of risk. No one should be surprised that risk is part of the initial discussion or ongoing processes.

3. Introduce a risk management survey.

When onboarding a new product or vendor or undertaking a new initiative, require a risk management survey that reviews how it would impact consumers and their data. This makes everyone take a step back to think about data security, compliance, and risk management, and share key information that can aid in monitoring, measuring, and mitigating risk.

4. Build trust and relationships with respect.

Many individual departments already have their own metrics and system for managing risk. When working to connect these departments, recognize what they have, the work they've put in, and bring that data to other departments to show where risks overlap with other departments. Trying to work with existing data and processes, particularly when they are generating strong results, goes a long way in creating an environment of respect.

5. Communicate.

Some people think the goal of ERM is to play "gotcha." In reality, ERM is a second line of defense. It's there to make processes safer and to add value. Demonstrate that value by showing how involving risk management from the beginning saves time on the backend. If a department tells risk management about an initiative late in the process or after the fact, the institution is missing the opportunity to evaluate and mitigate risk at the beginning, when it's easiest to make changes.

Done right, ERM can actually improve communication throughout the entire organization.

6. Reporting.

Reporting may feel like a finish line of sorts, but it's also an opportunity to educate. When reporting on risk, key stakeholders and decision makers should be present. Not only does proactively reviewing reports help keep an institution within its risk tolerance, it also ensures every business line and department is aware of what's going on around the institution.

Whether it's at a small institution where the same players are at the table for every discussion or a large one where committees rule risk, these tips simplify the daunting task of breaking down silos to ensure risk management is a shared duty.

When strategic planning is combined with quality risk information and analysis, it empowers an institution, giving it the tools to make smarter, more informed decisions. It's no wonder that institutions with strong enterprise risk management programs are valued 25 percent higher than those without them.[87] They have a culture where information is shared and data is regularly updated, giving the institution the opportunity to quickly adjust or pull back when indicators suggest a problem—or dig in and maximize an opportunity when risk is mitigated.

Long-term, consistent success requires playing the long game. Profitability isn't just about strategy for the next quarter, it is about managing the big picture and making strategic decisions today with a view towards what is down the road.

What does your institution envision for itself and its operational environment over the next few years? Does it see loan demand recovering? Opportunities in new markets? Innovative fintech partnerships or new technology initiatives? Plans to take customer service to the next level of excellence? A more complex compliance environment? Ongoing cybersecurity challenges? Rededication to business resiliency?

The only way to reach these goals and face these challenges is with foresight and planning. It's steering a course towards strategic success, knowing there will be bumps along the way. Your financial institution can't reach its goals if it doesn't follow its plan.

Going forward, enterprise risk management will continue to evolve in ways both expected and unexpected, as COSO has noted. As Big Data expands and more internal and external information becomes available, the ability to use advanced analytics will allow us to visualize risk in new ways, bringing both opportunities and overwhelming options. Artificial intelligence and automation may provide similar opportunities to discover hidden trends. As the need for ERM continues to grow, so do costs. Institutions will need to find ways to make ERM more ingrained into business processes in order to gain efficiencies and demonstrate value. Finally, better ERM will lead to stronger, better performing organizations by enabling earlier intervention when dealing with threats and opportunities.

Now is the time to think about how your risk management decisions are influencing your strategic planning. If the answer is that they aren't, ask yourself why. You may find that that status quo is riskier than you think.

ENDNOTES

[1] Farrell, Mark and Ronan Gallagher. The valuation implications of enterprise risk management maturity. Journal of Risk and Insurance. 82.3 (Sept. 2015): p625.

[2] St. Louis Fed Study Shows Community Bank Model Can Thrive In Good Times and In Bad" May 24, 2013. https://www.stlouisfed.org/news-re-leases/2013/05/24/st-louis-fed-study-shows-community-bank-model-can-thrive-in-good-times-and-in-bad

[3] Kahneman, D., & Tversky, A. (1982). Intuitive prediction: Biases and corrective procedures. In D. Kahneman, P. Slovic, & A. Tversky (Eds.), Judgment under Uncertainty: Heuristics and Biases (pp. 414-421). Cambridge: Cambridge University Press. doi:10.1017/CBO9780511809477.031

[4] Palmer, Charlie. The Middle Management Error Vendors Love the Most. June 20, 2017. http://adage.com/article/digitalnext/middle-management-error-vendors-love/309474/v

[5] Lencioni, Patrick M. Make Your Values Mean Something. Harvard Business Review. July 2002. https://hbr.org/2002/07/make-your-values-mean-something Accessed 12/1/17.

[6] Pasha, Shaheen and Seid, Jessica. Lay and Skilling's Day of Reckoning. CNNMoney. May 25, 2006. http://money.cnn.com/2006/05/25/news/newsmakers/enron_verdict/index.htm Accessed 12/4/17.

[7] Ibid.

[8] Barrionuevo, Alexei. Enron Chiefs Guilty of Fraud and Conspiracy. The New York Times. May 25, 2006. Accessed 12/4/17.

[9] Risk Management Principles for Third-Party Relationships. A Telephone Seminar for Community Banks. Handout. August 2002. https://www.occ.gov/static/past-conferences-and-seminars/vmts-final-handouts.pdf.

[10] The Risk Management Institute. A Risk Management Standard. 2002. https://www.theirm.org/media/4709/arms_2002_irm.pdf Accessed 1/29/2021.

[11] Srivastav, Shalini. A Study of Enterprise Risk Management in Banks. GYAN-PRATHA – ACCMAN Journal of Management. Volume 5. Issue 1. 2013

[12] Risk Appetite Statement. Office of the Comptroller of the Currency. November 2019. https://www.occ.treas.gov/publications/publications-by-type/other-publications-reports/risk-appetite-statement.pdf Accessed January 1, 2021.

[13] Executive Summary. Enterprise Risk Management—Integrating with Strategy and Performance. COSO. Page 17. June 2017. https://www.coso.org/Documents/2017-COSO-ERM-Integrating-with-Strategy-and-Performance-Executive-Summary.pdf Accessed 1/29/2021.

14 COSO 2013 Implementation Challenges. FDIC. 2016 Interagency Accounting Conference. March 15, 2016. https://www.fdic.gov/news/conferences/accounting/presentations/scallon-presentation-tuesday-march-15-1245pm-bw.pdf Accessed 10/15/17.

15 OCC 2003-12. Interagency Policy Statement on the Internal Audit Function and Its Outsourcing. Board of Governors of the Federal Reserve. Federal Deposit Insurance Corporation. Office of the Comptroller of the Currency. Office of Thrift Supervision. March 17, 2003. https://www.occ.gov/news-issuances/bulletins/2003/bulletin-2003-12a.pdf Accessed October 17, 2017.

16 NCUA Examiner Guide. Chapter 5. Supervisory Committee. https://www.ncua.gov/Legal/GuidesEtc/ExaminerGuide/Chapter05.pdf Accessed October 15, 2017.

17 Report: Majority Adopt New COSO Framework. Whitehouse, Tammy. Compliance Week. April 13, 2015. https://www.complianceweek.com/blogs/accounting-auditing-update/report-majority-adopt-new-coso-framework#.WeOgwmhSxPY Accessed 10/15/17.

18 The Fraud Triangle. Association of Certified Fraud Examiners. https://www.acfe.com/fraud-triangle.aspx Accessed 1/29/2021.

19 The Role of the Board of Directors in Enron's Collapse. Report prepared by Permanent Subcommittee on Investigations of the Committee on Governmental Affairs of the United States Senate. July 8, 2002.

20 The Rise and Fall of Enron. Thomas, William C. Journal of Accountancy. April 1, 2002. https://www.journalofaccountancy.com/issues/2002/apr/theriseandfallofenron.html Accessed 10/15/2017.

21 Supervisory Letter No.: 13-2. NCUA. Nov. 17, 2013.

22 Common Sense Approach to Community Banking. OCC. 2013. https://www.occ.gov/publications-and-resources/publications/banker-education/files/common-sense-approach-to-community-banking-.html Accessed March, 3, 2021.

23 Supervisory Guidance for Assessing Risk Management at Supervised Institutions with Total Consolidated Assets Less than $100 Billion. Federal Reserve Board. Updated 2/17/21. Accessed 3/6/21.

24 https://www.occ.gov/static/enforcement-actions/ea2020-056.pdf

25 https://www.federalreserve.gov/newsevents/pressreleases/files/enf20201007a1.pdf

26 OCC Semiannual Risk Perspective Fall 2019.

27 https://www.occ.gov/static/enforcement-actions/ea2020-036.pdf

[28] DEPARTMENT OF FINANCIAL SERVICES ANNOUNCES CYBERSECURITY CHARGES AGAINST A LEADING TITLE INSURANCE PROVIDER FOR EXPOSING MILLIONS OF DOCUMENTS WITH CONSUMERS' PERSONAL INFORMATION July 22, 2020. https://www.dfs.ny.gov/reports_and_publications/press_releases/pr202007221

[29] Institute of Internal Auditors. The Three Lines of Defense in Risk Management and Control. January 2013. https://na.theiia.org/standards-guidance/Public%20 Documents/PP%20The%20Three%20Lines%20of%20Defense%20in%20Effec-tive%20Risk%20Management%20and%20Control.pdf#:~:text=In%20the%20 Three%20Lines%20of,independent%20assurance%20is%20the%20third. Accessed 3/14/2021.

[30] OCC Assesses $250 Million Civil Money Penalty Against JPMorgan Chase Bank, N.A. Office of the Comptroller of the Currency. New Release 2020-159. November 24, 2020. https://www.occ.gov/news-issuances/news-releases/2020/nr-occ-2020-159.html Accessed 3/14/2021.

[31] Fintechs Continue to Drive Personal Loan Grwoth. TransUnion. February 21, 2019. https://newsroom.transunion.com/fintechs-continue-to-drive-personal-loans-to-record-levels/ Accessed January 3, 2021.

[32] VII. Unfair and Deceptive Practices — Third Party Risk. FDIC Consumer Compli-ance Examination Manual – June 2019. https://www.fdic.gov/regulations/compli-ance/manual/7/VII-4.1.pdf. Accessed 1/29/21.

[33] Opus & Ponemon Institute Announce Results of 2018 Third-Party Data Risk Study. November 15, 2018. https://apnews.com/press-release/pr-business-wire/556444d2cc114ea9a8ceda8f747b329c Accessed January 4, 2020.

[34] Larson, Selena. Verizon Data of 6 Million Users Leaked Online. CNN.com. July 12, 2017. http://money.cnn.com/2017/07/12/technology/verizon-data-leaked-online/index.html Accessed March 3, 2018.

[35] Technology Service Provider Contracts with FDIC-Supervised Institutions. FDIC Office of the Inspector General. February 2017. https://www.fdicoig.gov/pub-lications/technology-service-provider-contracts-fdic-supervised-institutions Accessed 1/29/2021.

[36] Docket No. 17-038-B-SM. Mid America Bank & Trust Company. Federal Reserve Consent Order. October 25, 2017. https://www.federalreserve.gov/newsevents/pressreleases/files/enf20171026a1.pdf Accessed March 3, 2018.

[37] Enforcement Action #2017-063. United States Department of the Treasury Comptroller of the Currency. August 1, 2017. https://www.occ.gov/static/enforce-ment-actions/ea2017-063.pdf Accessed March 3, 2018.

38 Consumer Financial Protection Bureau Orders Santander Bank to Pay $10 Million Fine for Illegal Overdraft Practices. July 14, 2016. CFPB. https://www.consumerfinance.gov/about-us/newsroom/consumer-financial-protection-bureau-orders-santander-bank-pay-10-million-fine-illegal-overdraft-practices/ Accessed March 3, 2018.

39 OCC's Semiannual Risk Perspective for Fall 2016. https://www.occ.treas.gov/publications/publications-by-type/other-publications-reports/semiannual-risk-perspective/semiannual-risk-perspective-fall-2016.pdf

40 Technology Service Provider Contracts with FDIC-Supervised Institutions. FDIC. February 2017. https://www.fdicoig.gov/publications/technology-service-provider-contracts-fdic-supervised-institutions Accessed 3/3/2021.

41 Ibid.

42 Ibid.

43 Apple Pay participating banks in Canada and the United States. Apple. https://support.apple.com/en-us/HT204916 Accessed January 3, 2021.

44 Hiltzik, Michael. So Much for the Claim That Apple Pay Would Be 'Secure.' The Los Angeles Times. March 7, 2015. http://www.latimes.com/business/hiltzik/la-fi-mh-apple-pay-would-be-secure-20150307-column.html Accessed February 25, 2018.

45 Fox-Brewster, Thomas. Here's Proof Apple Pay Is Useful for Stealing People's Money. Forbes. March 1, 2016. https://www.forbes.com/sites/thomasbrewster/2016/03/01/apple-pay-fraud-test/#2e1c1e4a46c6 Accessed March 3, 2018.

46 Kitten, Tracy. Apple Pay: Fraudsters Exploit Authentication. Bank Info Security. March 2, 2015. http://www.bankinfosecurity.com/apple-pay-fraudsters-exploit-authentication-a-7967 Accessed March 3, 2018.

47 Thompson, Cadie. How Hackers Could Still Get Around Apple Pay Security. CNBC. September 11, 2014. https://www.cnbc.com/2014/09/11/how-hackers-could-still-get-around-apple-pay-security.html Accessed March 3, 2018.

48 FinCEN Assesses $1 Million Penalty and Seeks to Bar Former MoneyGram Executive from Financial Industry. FinCEN. December 18, 2014. https://www.fincen.gov/news/news-releases/fincen-assesses-1-million-penalty-and-seeks-bar-former-moneygram-executive. Accessed March 3, 2018.

49 Former Bank Teller Pleads Guilty to Federal Charge For Stealing More Than $185,000 From Homeless Customer. United States Department of Justice. September 28, 2017. https://www.justice.gov/usao-dc/pr/former-bank-teller-pleads-guilty-federal-charge-stealing-more-185000-homeless-customer Accessed March 3, 2018.

[50] Nogami, Tatsuya. Reexamination of the Association Between Anonymity and Self-Interested Unethical Behavior in Adults. The Psychological record, 2009, 59, 259–272.

[51] WALL STREET AND THE FINANCIAL CRISIS: Anatomy of a Financial Collapse. MAJORITY AND MINORITY STAFF REPORT. PERMANENT SUBCOMMITTEE ON INVESTIGATIONS. United States Senate. April 13, 2011.

[52] The Hazards of Expert Control: Chief Risk Officers and Risky Derivatives. Kim Pernell, Jiwook Jung, Frank Dobbin. American Sociological Review. Vol 82, Issue 3, pp. 511 – 541. May 31, 2017.

[53] Research: Hiring Chief Risk Officers Led Banks to Take on Even More Risk. Pernell, Kim, Jiwood Jong, and Frank Dobbin. Harvard Business Review. July 13, 2017.

[54] Consumer Financial Protection Bureau Fines Wells Fargo $100 Million for Widespread Illegal Practice of Secretly Opening Unauthorized Accounts. CFPB. September 8, 2016. https://www.consumerfinance.gov/about-us/newsroom/consumer-financial-protection-bureau-fines-wells-fargo-100-million-widespread-illegal-practice-secretly-opening-unauthorized-accounts/

[55] Wells Fargo's (WFC) Management Presents at Barclays Global Financial Services Conference (Transcript). Seeking Alpha. September, 13, 2016. https://seekingalpha.com/article/4005960-wells-fargos-wfc-management-presents-barclays-global-financial-services-conference-transcript

[56] Farrell, Mark and Ronan Gallagher. The valuation implications of enterprise risk management maturity. Journal of Risk and Insurance. 82.3 (Sept. 2015): p625.

[57] #2017-047 OFFICE OF THE COMPTROLLER OF THE CURRENCY CONSENT ORDER. June 18, 2017. https://www.occ.gov/static/enforcement-actions/ea2017-047.pdf

[58] #N16-002 OFFICE OF THE COMPTROLLER OF THE CURRENCY NOTICE OF CHARGES FOR PROHIBITION AND RESTITUTION AND NOTICE OF ASSESSMENT OF CIVIL MONEY PENALTY. June 30, 2016. https://www.occ.gov/static/enforcement-actions/eaN16-002.pdf

[59] Patrick, Margot. "The $500 Million Central Bank Heist—and How It Was Foiled." The Wall Street Journal. 10/3/2018. Accessed 1/1/2021.

[60] http://www.ey.com/Publication/vwLUAssets/ey-shifting-focus-risk-culture-at-the-forefront-of-banking/$FILE/ey-shifting-focus-risk-culture-at-the-forefront-of-banking.pdf

[61] CFTC Orders Barclays to pay $200 Million Penalty for Attempted Manipulation of and False Reporting concerning LIBOR and Euribor Benchmark Interest Rates. U.S. Commodities Futures Trading Commission press release. June 27, 2012. http://www.cftc.gov/PressRoom/PressReleases/pr6289-12 Accessed 10/15/2017.

[62] Salz Review. An Independent View of Barclays' Business Practices. Anthony Salz. April 2013. https://www.home.barclays/content/dam/barclayspublic/documents/news/875-269-salz-review-04-2013.pdf Accessed 10/15/2017.

[63] CFTC

[64] Thomas, C. William. The Rise and Fall of Enron. Journal of Accountancy. April 2002. Pgs 41-48.

[65] Ibid.

[66] Labaton Sucharow. United States & United Kimgdom Financial Services Industry Survey July 2012. www.labaton.com/en/about/press/upload/US-UK-Financial-Services-Industry-Survey.pdf Accessed February 21, 2018.

[67] https://www2.deloitte.com/content/dam/Deloitte/uk/Documents/financial-services/deloitte-uk-culture-in-banking.pdf

[68] https://files.consumerfinance.gov/f/documents/201701_cfpb_TCF-National-Bank-complaint.pdf

[69] Bureau of Consumer Financial Protection Settles With TCF National Bank. CFPB. July 20, 2018. https://www.consumerfinance.gov/about-us/newsroom/bureau-consumer-financial-protection-settles-tcf-national-bank/ Accessed January 3, 2021.

[70] William C. Dudley. Reforming Culture for the Long Term. Remarks at the Banking Standards Board, London, United Kingdom. March 21, 2017. https://www.newyorkfed.org/newsevents/speeches/2017/dud170321 Accessed February 21, 2018.

[71] PwC's 2017 Risk in review study: Managing risk from the frontline. https://www.pwc.com/us/en/risk-assurance/risk-in-review-study/survey-findings-risk-culture.html Accessed: February 20, 2018.

[72] Deloitte Touche Tohmatsu Limited. The Leadership Premium. March 2012. https://www2.deloitte.com/content/dam/Deloitte/global/Documents/Human-Capital/dttl-hc-leadershippremium-8092013.pdf. Accessed December 21, 2018.

[73] 2019 North American Pulse of Internal Audit. The Institute of Internal Auditors. https://www.theiia.org/centers/aec/Pages/2019-Pulse-of-Internal-Audit.aspx Accessed 3/4/21.

[74] https://ithandbook.ffiec.gov/it-booklets/information-security/ii-information-security-program-management/iic-risk-mitigation/iic5-inventory-and-classification-of-assets.aspx

[75] Appendix A: Examination Procedures https://ithandbook.ffiec.gov/it-booklets/information-security/ii-information-security-program-management/iic-risk-mitigation/iic5-inventory-and-classification-of-assets.aspx

[76] https://ithandbook.ffiec.gov/it-booklets/management/iii-it-risk-management/iiia-risk-identification.aspx

[77] Digital Banking Users to Reach Nearly 3 Billion By 2021, Representing 1 In 2 Global Adult Population. Juniper Research. February 8, 2017. https://www.juniperresearch.com/press/press-releases/digital-banking-users-to-reach-nearly-3-billion-by.

[78] Andriotis, AnnaMaria and Julia Haslanger. What Customers Want from Their Banks: Ease. June 3, 2016. https://www.wsj.com/articles/what-customers-want-from-their-banks-ease-1464980843

[79] Juniper Research.

[80] Deitrick, Calla. Smartphone thefts drop as kill switch usage grows. Consumer Reports. June 11, 2015. http://www.consumerreports.org/cro/news/2015/06/smartphone-thefts-on-the-decline/index.htm.

[81] More Americans Use PINs and Passwords to Protect Personal Data on Smartphones and Tablets in 2015 than 2012. CTIA. https://www.ctia.org/news/more-americans-use-pins-and-passwords-to-protect-personal-data-on-smartphones-and-tablets-in-2015-than-in-2012 Accessed 3/4/21.

[82] Federal Financial Institutions Examination Council Bank Secrecy Act/Anti-Money Laundering InfoBase. BSA/AML Risk Assessment-Overview. https://www.ffiec.gov/bsa_aml_infobase/pages_manual/olm_005.htm Accessed 11/16/2017.

[83] Federal Reserve Bank of St. Louis. St. Louis Fed Study Shows Community Bank Model Can Thrive In Good Times and In Bad. 5/24/2013. https://www.stlouisfed.org/news-releases/2013/05/24/st-louis-fed-study-shows-community-bank-model-can-thrive-in-good-times-and-in-bad Accessed 3/14/2021.

[84] PowerPoint Presentation (coso.org)

[85] https://www.mckinsey.com/~/media/mckinsey/featured%20insights/leadership/the%20board%20perspective/the-board-perspective.ashx

86 St. Louis Fed Study Shows Community Bank Model Can Thrive In Good Times and In Bad" May 24, 2013. https://www.stlouisfed.org/news-releases/2013/05/24/st-louis-fed-study-shows-community-bank-model-can-thrive-in-good-times-and-in-bad

87 Farrell, Mark and Ronan Gallagher. The valuation implications of enterprise risk management maturity. Journal of Risk and Insurance. 82.3 (Sept. 2015): p625.

INDEX